新文科思政教程 NEW LIBERAL ARTS IDEOLOGICAL
AND POLITICAL COURSE

语言学导论

INTRODUCTION TO LINGUISTICS

黄睿　杜磊◎著

新华出版社

图书在版编目（CIP）数据

语言学导论 / 黄睿, 杜磊著.

－－ 北京：新华出版社, 2023.9

ISBN 978－7－5166－7017－0

Ⅰ.①语…　Ⅱ.①黄…　②杜…　Ⅲ.①语言学　Ⅳ.①H0

中国国家版本馆CIP数据核字（2023）第174228号

语言学导论

作　者： 黄　睿　杜　磊

责任编辑： 时光慧　　　　　　　　　**封面设计：** 刘宝龙

出版发行： 新华出版社

地　址： 北京石景山区京原路8号　　　　**邮　编：** 100040

网　址： http://www.xinhuapub.com

经　销： 新华书店、新华出版社天猫旗舰店、京东旗舰店及各大网店

购书热线： 010－63077122　　　**中国新闻书店购书热线：** 010－63072012

照　排： 六合方圆

印　刷： 北京明恒达印务有限公司

成品尺寸： 170mm×240mm　1/16

印　张： 15　　　　　　　　　　　**字　数：** 178千字

版　次： 2023年10月第一版　　　　　**印　次：** 2023年10月第一次印刷

书　号： ISBN 978－7－5166－7017－0

定　价： 39.00元

前　言

　　本教材参照国家新文科建设和《普通高等学校本科外国语言文学类专业教学指南（2020 年版）》的要求，助力《语言学导论》课程的新文科教材建设和英语专业课程思政教学。以传统英语语言学概论课程内容为主体，参考经典语言学书目，并借鉴了当前语言学流派的观点与共识，同时结合作者十几年的教学经验，形成了一本传统与新颖相连接、理论与实践共融合的教材。

　　本教材章节框架简明、清晰、体现语言学研究主要成果和前沿趋势；章节内容准确、扼要，能够满足学生考研实际需求；各章节知识、能力和素质点明确，为英语专业学习奠定语言知识基础；各章节引用英汉语言典型案例，培养学生对语言研究的兴趣，加深理论理解和英汉对比意识，提升学生的文化自信和优秀中华文化外宣意识和能力，实现"盐溶于水"的课程思政教学目的和立德树人的根本目标。

　　本教材为语言学本体内容，分为六章。第一章介绍语言、语言学、语言学主要流派及汉语的语言学研究。第二章语音学和音系学介绍国际音标图、英语元音和辅音的发音及描述、汉语拼音和超音段特征。第三章形态学介绍词、屈折变化和构词法、典型汉语构词法和案例，以及词汇层面的中西文化交流。第四章句法介绍英语传统句法、结构主义句法和功能主义句法，以及典型汉语句法和案例。第五章语义学介绍对意义的研究、词和句子的主要意义关系，以及汉语语义学研究和文化。第六章语用学介绍语境、语用学（区别于句法学／语义学）、言语行为理论、会话含义和礼貌原则，以及汉语语用学研究和礼貌文化。

目录
Contents

目录
Contents

Chapter 6 Pragmatics: The Use of Language in Context ············· **175**

Chapter 1

Language and Linguistics

语 言 学 导 论
新文科思政教程

1.1 Introduction

Language is something we use every day that we almost take it for granted just like our five senses which are functions of our organs. Yet the fact is that even we have speech organs, we still need constant language input in specific cultural environment at appropriate time to nurture our speaking ability. That is why some babies acquire a second language when grow up in a foreign country and some babies lose their ability to speak when isolated from human communities.

The linguistic study of language needs a systematic learning. As a common communication tool, language reflects common human thought and cognition, for example *at the foot of the mountain, bottleneck.* But more chances are we would encounter obstacles in cross-language communication. English majors should enhance their mastering of English and Chinese to get a clear idea of the nature and basic discipline of language, to know the difference between Chinese and English, and to touch the cutting edge of linguistic study. That is the aim of this course book which will benefit English majors.

Learning Objectives:

1. Remember the following terms: language; design features of language; functions of language; definition of linguistics and its research principles; major distinctions in linguistics

2. Understand: differences between modern linguistics and traditional grammar

3. Illustrate with examples: design features of language; functions of language

4. Tell examples: about cultural transmission in Chinese language

Lead-in Questions:

1. What is language? E.g. how to translate: "-What's this? -It is an apple", Adam's apple, the apple in one's eye, 没门儿, 丈夫, 物联网, etc.

2. Watch the video clips "Pride and Prejudice"(Darcy's expression of love to Elizabeth), 电影《刘三姐》（对歌片段）, and discuss functions of language.

3. Discuss culture backgrounds for typical phatic communions in Chinese, English and a third language.

1.2 Language

Even we live with language every day, it is hard to make a clear definition of language all at once. The language we focus on is human language in general instead of any other language such as animal language, and machine language. The following are famous linguists' definition of language:

According to Sapir (1921), "language is a purely human and non-instinctive method of communicating ideas, emotions and desires by means of voluntarily produced symbols."

According to Bloch and Trager (1942), "a language is a system of arbitrary vocal symbols by means of which a social group cooperates."

Chomsky (1957) points out that a language is "a set (finite or infinite) of sentences, each finite in length and constructed out of a finite set of elements."

Halliday describes language as a semiotic system, "not in the sense of a system of signs, but a systemic resource for meaning". For Halliday, language is a "meaning potential"; by extension, he defines linguistics as the study of "how people exchange meanings by 'languaging'" (https://en.wikipedia.org/wiki/Michael_Halliday).

Try to find the commonalities and differences between the above definitions, and get your definition of language.

1.2.1 Definition of Language

Based on the linguists' study of language, a generally acceptable definition is: language is a system of arbitrary vocal symbols used for human communication. There are five key words in the definition of language: system, vocal, arbitrary, symbol and human.

1.2.2 Design Features of Language

Language is human specific. To summarize the design features of language which distinguish it from any other communication means can help us better understand the nature of human language. American structural linguist C. F. Hockett (1958) proposed 16 key features of human language: vocal–auditory channel, broadcast transmission and directional reception, transitoriness, interchangeability, total feedback, specialization, semanticity, arbitrariness, discreteness, displacement, productivity, cultural transmission, duality, prevarication, reflexiveness, and learnability. Among them, 5 are generally acknowledged as design features of human language.

Arbitrariness

Saussure (1916) pointed out the arbitrary nature between the signifier and the signified in human language — between the sound or shape of a word and the concept to which it refers. Arbitrariness means the forms of linguistic signs bear no natural relationship to their meaning. The link between them is a matter of convention, and conventions differ across languages. So, languages differ from each other in naming all the things in the world. Shakespeare pointed out that "A rose by any other name would smell as sweet." (*Romeo and Juliet*).

Opposite to arbitrariness as a basic nature of language, we find motivation in different levels of language, for example, Chinese ideographs, onomatopoeia, compound words, different sentence arrangements, and etc.

Widdowson (1996: 6) illustrated arbitrariness of onomatopoeic word by changing "murmurous" into "murderous" in a line from Keats' *Ode to a Nightingale*: "The murmurous haunt of flies on summer eves". The change of the onomatopoeic word "murmurous" into another one with similar sound — "murderous" makes the meaning totally different. Even onomatopoeic words imitate sounds in the world, Widdowson pointed out its arbitrary nature.

Duality

Duality refers to the property of having two levels of structures, such that units of the primary level are composed of elements of the secondary level and each of the two levels has its own principles of organization (Lyons, 1981: 20). At the higher level, language can be primarily analyzed in terms of combinations of meaningful units (words and morphemes), and secondarily analyzed in terms of meaningless segments (phonemes). For instance, *She comes from Italy*, at the first higher level, the sentence consists of meaningful units, *she, come, −s* (a morpheme indicating third person singular number), *from, Italy*. At the lower level, theses meaningful units are made up of phonological units, /ʃ/, /iː/, /k/, /ʌ/, /m/, /z/, etc. As individual sounds, these units are meaningless in themselves. All communication systems can deliver meaning, but are not necessarily composed of two levels of units like human language. Duality enables language users to produce numerous forms by combining a limited number of language sounds in various ways.

Productivity

Due to its duality and its recursiveness, language is resourceful. Productivity or creativity means the creative capacity of language users to produce and understand an infinitely large number of sentences, including those they have never heard before.

The recursive nature of language theoretically provides a potential to create endless sentences, for example, *Dorothy thinks that Toto suspects that Tin Man said that ...*

Displacement

Displacement is a property of language enabling its users to talk about things which are not present (in time and place) at the moment of communication. Thus, we say: *Xi'an is an ancient city which brings us back to the Qin Dynasty. When face–to–face meeting is impossible, there is always the possibility of having everything online.* Displacement enables language users to make generalization and abstraction. We can talk about beauty and truth. Whereas most animals communicate as a response to an immediate stimulus, for example, monkey's warning cry, honeybee's dance, and ants' scent and touch.

Cultural Transmission

Language is not genetically inherited. Passed from generation to generation, it requires some learning. It is true human are born with language capacity ("language acquisition device" by N. Chomsky, LAD). But the particular language a person learns to speak is a cultural one rather than a genetic one like the dog's barking system. Human infants will lose their power of human language if they grow up in isolation from any language–speaking community.

1.2.3 Origin of Language

Writing is not language, but merely a way of recording language by means of visible marks (Bloomfield, 2002: 20). Language begins far earlier in its oral mode. The shortage of direct, empirical evidence has caused many scholars to regard the entire topic of the origin of language as unsuitable for serious study; in 1866, the Linguistic Society of Paris banned any existing or future debates on the subject, a prohibition which remained influential across much of the Western world until late in the 20th century (https://en.wikipedia.org/wiki/Origin_of_language). There are some well-known theories about the origin of language. The following are some of them:

The bow-wow or cuckoo theory sees early words as imitations of the cries of beasts and birds. Onomatopoeic words seem to be evidence for this theory. But onomatopoeic words are also under specific social conventions: a dog *barks* in English; while "汪汪" in Chinese.

The pooh-pooh theory sees the first words as emotional interjections and exclamations triggered by pain, pleasure, surprise, etc. There are interjections in language as evidence for this theory. The problem is that interjections also have social boundaries: A Briton "ouch"! A Chinese "哎呦"!

The yo-he-ho theory claims language emerged from human rhythmic grunts when working together, such as sounds of "yo-he-ho". Yet, these primitive rhythmic grunts are a little far away from rhythms of human language, such as poems and songs.

The above speculations on the origin of language do not explain the evolvement of language as a social, cultural and psychological phenomenon, but they reflect people's concern of humanity.

* 中英语言文化：语言的起源

*1. 中国文化：

《易·系辞下》："上古结绳而治，后世圣人易之以书契。"

《荀子·解蔽》："故好书者众矣，而仓颉独传者，壹也。"

《淮南子·本经训》："昔者仓颉作书，而天雨粟，鬼夜哭。"

许慎《说文解字叙》："黄帝之史仓颉，见鸟兽蹄远之迹，知分理之可相别异也，初造书契。百工以乂，万品以察，盖取诸夬。""仓颉之初作书也，盖依类象形，故谓之文。其后形声相益，即谓之字。"

	甲骨文	金文	小篆	隶书	草书	行书	楷书
火							火
日							日
月							月
山							山
田							田

汉字的演变（有观点认为汉字字体演变顺序为：甲骨文、金文、小篆、隶书、楷书、草书、行书，本教材采用王力的观点）

上古结绳、仓颉造字的中国神话反映了人们对于汉字起源的一种信仰。文献研究表明，汉字起源于距今 6000 年左右的仰韶文化；成体系于夏代的中、晚期（距今 3800—3600 年）。人民大众是汉字的创造者。秦始皇统一中国，汉字以小篆的形式固定下来（陈炜湛，1978）。

大致说，汉语的古今字体只有两大类：第一类是刀笔文字，其笔画粗细如一，不能为撇捺；第二类是毛笔文字，其笔画能为撇捺，粗细随意。甲骨文、金文、小篆等都属于第一类，隶书、草书、行书、楷书等都属于第二类。

甲骨文是"龟甲兽骨文字"的简称，又叫"殷墟文字、殷契卜辞"等。它是殷代的人用刀刻在龟甲或兽骨上的关于卜卦的文字。甲骨文是殷代王朝所用的，字体和金文稍有出入。现在我们所能看见的是商王盘庚从黄河以南迁到黄河以北的时候起到商纣亡国的时候的甲骨文字（约公元前 1401 年—公元前 1122 年）。

金文，原来叫作"钟鼎文"，因为这种文字多数刻在鼎上和钟上。后来大家觉得不限于钟鼎，所以改称金文。古人把铜铁都叫作"金"，金文实际上是刻在铜器上的文字。刻在铜器上这种行为叫作"铭"，所以金文又称"铭文"。金文大约是吉祥的话（吉金）、庆功的话或自勉的话。金文的时代是从商代到六朝，共两千多年。但引起文字学家最大兴趣的只是先秦的金文。

战国时代，列国割据，文字不能统一。所以许慎《说文解字序》里说："言语共声，文字异形。"秦始皇统一天下，统一文字——小篆。隶书的创造是中国文字史上的一大改革，"秦……大发吏卒，兴役戍，官狱职务繁，初有隶书，以趣约易"。可见隶书是应实际需要而产生的。写字工具的改变，大大地影响字体的改革，相传蒙恬造笔，蒙恬正是秦代的人。造笔和造字一样，都是人民的创造，不能说是蒙恬个人的发明。但是说秦代才有毛笔是近于事实的，先秦书籍中没有"笔"字。也可能是战国时代已经有了毛笔，但不如秦汉那样广泛应用。有了毛笔，文字的姿态大大地改变了。秦代虽有隶书，但是不作为正式的文字。秦始皇在各处刻石，都用的是小篆。到了汉代，隶书渐渐变成正式文字，连刻碑也用隶书了。此后两千年中间不曾有过很大的改革，汉字的字体和字式都基本上固定下来了。隶书是为简易而创造的，此风一开，大家便向简易的道路上走去，于是有了草书。现在我们所能看见的草书是汉建武三十年（公元54年）的木简。草书是尽可能把隶书每字的笔画连接起来成为一两笔。学会了隶书的人不一定能看懂草书。写字的方便带来了别人认字的麻烦，于是又产生了行书。行书可以说是把隶书简化了而又参用草书笔画的一种文字。楷书是汉字字体的最后形式。楷书只是隶书的变体，所以有人叫作"今隶"。从字式来说，楷书和隶书的分别甚微。从字体来说，区别也不大，只是把横书改为收锋，把撇捺改为斜下或翘上罢了。由隶书到楷书是字体的第二阶段，可以叫作"毛笔阶段"（王力，2015: 39–41）。

*2. Bible (Genesis):

"And Cush begat Nimrod: he began to be a mighty one in the earth. He was a mighty hunter before the LORD: wherefore it is said, Even as Nimrod the mighty hunter before the LORD. And the beginning of his kingdom was Babel, and Erech, and Accad, and Calneh, in the land of Shinar." (https://www.biblegateway.com/passage/?search=Genesis+10&version=KJV)

"And the whole earth was of one language, and of one speech. And it came to pass, as they journeyed from the east, that they found a plain in the land of Shinar; and they dwelt there. And they said one to another, Go to, let us make brick, and burn them thoroughly. And they had brick for stone, and slime had they for morter. And they said, Go to, let us build us a city and a tower, whose top may reach unto heaven; and let us make us a name, lest we be scattered abroad upon the face of the whole earth. And the Lord came down to see the city and the tower, which the children of men builded. And the Lord said, Behold, the people is one, and they have all one language; and this they begin to do: and now nothing will be restrained from them, which they have imagined to do. Go to, let us go down, and there confound their language, that they may not understand

Pieter Bruegel's *The Tower of Babel* depicts a traditional Nimrod inspecting stonemasons.(https://en.wikipedia.org/wiki/Nimrod)

one another's speech. So the Lord scattered them abroad from thence upon the face of all the earth: and they left off to build the city. Therefore is the name of it called Babel; because the Lord did there confound the language of all the earth: and from thence did the Lord scatter them abroad upon the face of all the earth."(https://www.biblegateway.com/passage/?search=Genesis%2011%3A1–9&version=KJV)

1.2.4 Functions of Language

The primary function of language is its informative function which enables us record facts, and exchange ideas. Everyone can list functions of language by his own experience and understanding of language. Famous linguists' theories can help us get a broad classification of the basic functions of language.

For Jakobson, a pioneer structural linguist of the Prague School, language is above all for communication. In his famous article *Linguistics and Poetics* (1960), Jakobson defined the 6 key factors of human speech communication: context, message, addresser, addressee, contact, and code. Based on these 6 key factors of speech communication, Jakobson established his well-known framework of language functions.

Functions:

1. referential: contextual information

2. poetic: auto-reflection

3. emotive: self-expression

4. conative: vocative or imperative addressing of receiver

5. phatic: checking channel working

6. metalingual: checking code working

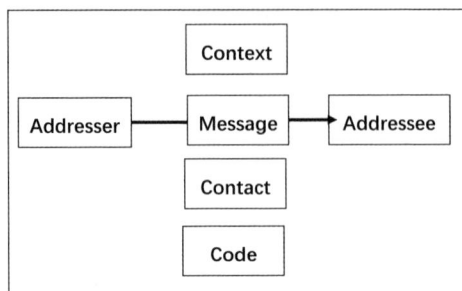

Besides, Halliday the founder of Systemic–Functional Grammar proposes a theory of metafunctions of language comprising ideational, interpersonal and textual functions. Ideational function constructs a model of experience as well as logical relations; interpersonal function enacts social relationships; and textual function creates relevance to context (Halliday, 1994).

Based on the common recognition and further concerned topics of linguistics, we list the following basic functions of language:

Informative

Language is an instrument of thought, and it records the facts. *Water boils at 100℃. The earth revolves around the sun.* The use of language to record the facts is a prerequisite of social development.

It equals Halliday's ideational function of language that serves for the expression of content: that is, of the speaker's experience of the real world, including the inner world of his own consciousness.

Phatic Function /Communion

People use small, seemingly meaningless expressions (ritual of greeting and farewell) to establish or maintain a comfortable relationship between the speaker and the hearer without involving any factual content.

The term Phatic Communion was put forward by anthropologist Malinowski (1923) in his essay *The Problem of Meaning in Primitive Language* as a supplementary contribution to C. K. Ogden and I. A. Richards' book *The Meaning of Meaning*. He pointed out the importance of socia-cultural context in understanding the primitive language. He found phatic communion "serves to establish bonds of personal union between people brought together by the mere need of companionship and does not serve any purpose of communicating ideas" (1923: 316). Phatic communion is a common function of language in both primitive and civilized speech communities.

Interpersonal Function

Interpersonal function is the most important sociological use of language, by which people establish and maintain their social status in a society. There is a proverb in both Chinese and English that "our speech will betray us", which unveils a truth that language marks our identity, physically in terms of age, sax, and voiceprints; psychologically in terms of language, personality, and intelligence; geographically in terms of accents and dialects; ethnically in terms of social stratification, class, status, role, solidarity and distance (Crystal,

1992: 17). For example, the address terms, cheerleading slogans, and so on. Interpersonal function of language is also in line with specific social and cultural convention.

Performative Function

Besides making exchange of information, we can do things with words. The concept of performative function originates from Austin and Searle's philosophical study of language, which forms the backbone of pragmatics. The performative function of language is primarily to change the social status of persons, as in signing a business deal, making a staff appointment, the sentencing of criminals, and Western marriage ceremony.

The language used is formal and ritualized. The ritualized procedure should be fulfilled to achieve the performative function. For example, only authoritative person has the power to declare the opening of Olympic Games.

The language used also reflects cultural features. A couple normally get their marriage certificates before the wedding ceremony in China; while in Christian countries, they get recognized by the priest at the wedding ceremony. Wedding customs are different in China and the West.

Emotive Function

The emotive function enables language users to change the emotional status of an audience for or against someone or something. According to Crystal (1992: 17), it is a means of getting rid of our nervous energy when we are under stress, e.g. exclamations or interjections conveying human emotions or as an involuntary verbal reaction to a sensational or psychological stimulus such as physical pain, beautiful scenery, e.g. *Ouch, Splendid, Cool, Damn it, What a sight, Wow, Hurray, Shit.*

Recreational Function

The recreational function of language refers to human use of language for the sheer joy of using it. It is close to Jakobson's poetic function. Like art for art's sake, human beings have enjoyed the joy of using language itself since long ago, such as 对歌，对诗，对联 in ancient Chinese. Poems, riddles, and verbal duels in both English and Chinese today are live examples demonstrating human joy of using language.

Metalingual Function

Human language can be used to talk about itself. Language is self-reflexive. We can talk about talk and think about thinking, and thus only human can ask what it means to communicate, to think. To organize any written text into a coherent whole, writers employ certain expressions to keep their readers informed about where they are and where they are going, for example, *to tell the truth, frankly speaking, as a matter of fact, to be precise, in other words, that is to say, etc.*

1.2.5 Contrast of Chinese and English

1. 请查找以下汉语 / 英语表达承载的文化意义，如何翻译：

万古长青、青红皂白、青花瓷、名垂青史、青睐、垂青、青丝

绿水青山就是金山银山

姹紫嫣红、红运、红人、网红、红包、红娘、分红、赤字、红领巾、又红又专、红眼病、红牌、红灯区、红十字

黑科技、数字经济、虚拟教研室

white lie, white-collar, dark horse, black coffee, black sheep, green hand, green policy, green with envy, red states and blue states, in the red, blues

没门儿、东西、江南、丈夫

2. 不同语言的不同寒暄方式反映了不同的文化背景。请查找英语 "It is a nice day today." 和汉语"吃了吗"背后的文化故事。其他语言文化如何寒暄？寒暄方式有时代差异吗？

3. 请对比以下英汉脑筋急转弯这一言语幽默在英汉语言中的表达异同点。

— 如何形容世界上最繁忙的机场？ — 日理万机。

— 谁最喜欢咬文嚼字？ — 蛀书虫。

— 金先生一向心直口快，是什么事让他突然变得吞吞吐吐了？

— 金先生在抽烟的时候吞吞吐吐。

— Which hand should you stir soup with? — Neither, you should use a spoon.

— At what time of day was Adam born? — A little before Eve.

— What's black and white and red/ read all over? — A newspaper.

4. 据参考消息网 5 月 10 日报道，现在流行把让人叹为观止的新科技称为"黑科技"。"百度"和"有道"对"黑科技"的翻译都是 black technology。其实这样直译是错误的。根据《韦氏词典》释义，与中文的"黑"类似，black 可用来形容阴险、被谴

责以及邪恶的东西，因此 black technology 会让人想到服务于恶势力的科技。Technode.com 网站曾发表文章 There's Nothing Dark Or Evil About "Black Technology"（"黑科技"无关邪恶），澄清中国人所说的"黑科技"是褒扬而非谴责。文章第一段说道：If your technology is described as "black" in China, don't be offended…Unlike black magic, it has nothing to do with voodooism or malicious enchantment, but rather a term reserved for only the most mind-boggling，futuristic and out-of-this-world scientific feats（如果你的科技在中国被称为"黑科技"，不要不高兴……与黑魔法不同，"黑科技"与巫毒教以及邪恶妖术无关。这个词只用来形容最惊人、富有未来感和超越这个世界的科学成就）。与其让别人澄清，不如我们自己在翻译的时候考虑得更全面一些。

把"黑科技"译为 black technology 还可能引发另一种误解。美国有线电视新闻网曾在其网站上发表文章称：But obtaining information about today's black technology applications is virtually impossible. In official circles, a black program may be classified as "deniable", which means people can refute that the government is developing or knows about its existence（但想要了解今天的黑色科技几乎是不可能的。对官方来说，黑色项目或归于"可否认"一类，也就是说官员可以否认政府正在从事或了解相关研发）。这里的 black technology 是指政府秘密进行的研发工作。

笔者认为"黑科技"可译为 futuristic tech，或更直接些译为 cool tech。这类译法虽缺少特色，但起码不会引发歧义。(http://www.cankaoxiaoxi.com/ym/20170510/1978196.shtml)。

1.3 Linguistics

Linguistics is usually defined as the science of language or, alternatively, as the scientific study of language (Lyons, 1981: 37). Linguistics builds on the past, not only by challenging and refuting traditional doctrines but also by developing and reformulating them. With the development of AI, language-related industries such as machine translation, robot, website designing, language teaching and other language service industries boom. It is easier for us to accept linguistics as a scientific study of language. The early 20th century saw a beginning of modern linguistics when a systematic study of language gained its independence from other social sciences. In the early new century, it has advanced to such an interdisciplinary stage that it has been classified as a social science, natural science, cognitive science, or part of the humanities (https://en.wikipedia.org/wiki/Linguistics).

Concerning its methodology, linguistics is always guided by the 4 principles of science: 1) exhaustiveness: it strives to leave no stone unturned for the defined subject; 2) consistency: there should be no contradiction between different parts of the statement; 3) economy: the statement should be concise rather than redundant; and 4) objectivity: there should be no prejudice against any minor language phenomenon and the linguistic study is impartial and descriptive. Linguistic study bases itself upon a systematic investigation of language data which aims at discovering the true nature of language and its underlying system. To make sense of the data, a linguist usually tries to conceive and then formulate some hypothesis about the language structure. And then the hypothesis will be checked against the observed or observable facts to test its validity.

Data   collection   —>   tentative   rule   construction   —>   tentative   rule examination —> rule finalization.

Modern linguistics is different from traditional grammar in the following aspects:

1) Descriptive vs. Prescriptive

"To say that linguistics is a descriptive (i.e. non—normative) science is to say that the linguist tries to discover and record the rules to which the members of a language community actually conform and does not seek to impose upon them other (i.e. extraneous) rules, or norms, of correctness" (Lyons, 1981: 47).

The publication of Ferdinand de Saussure's *Course in General Linguistics* in 1906 was the starting point of structural linguistics, an approach to linguistics that flourished in Europe and the United States in the first half of the 20th century. From the 1930's to the 1950's, the American linguists L. Bloomfield and E. Sapir, who reexamined the ideas of the neogrammarian doctrine, founded a new trend of linguistics— descriptive linguistics.

The previous study of language (e.g. Latin, French) in Europe was mainly prescriptive. The grammarians tried to lay down rules for the correct use of language and settle the disputes over usage once and for all.

```
Do/ Don't say X!

People do/ don't say X.
```

As a scientific study of language, modern linguistics is preoccupied with describing the facts of language usage. It does not mean there is no room for prescription at all, such as "There are obvious administrative and education advantages, in the modern world, in standardizing the principal dialect that is employed within a particular country or region" (Lyons, 1981: 53).

2) Spoken Language vs. Written Language

Traditional grammar mainly lays down rules in written language, so written language plays an important role in the traditional study of language. Whereas, modern linguistics regards spoken language as the primary medium of language which is more important.

3) (No) Latin-Based Framework

Traditional grammar in Europe mostly takes Latin grammar as a framework to lay down rules for people to follow. Yule (2000: 95) noted the fact that Latin infinitives are single words and just do not split; while the infinitive in English has the form *to + the verb*. English is not the same as Latin. This mismatch produced such ridiculous grammar rules, e.g. *You must not split an infinitive*. In contrast, modern linguistics does not impose Latin grammar on other languages, and adopts an objective and descriptive approach in language study.

1.3.1 The Scope of Linguistics

Concerning the scope of linguistics, we had better first make a distinction between general linguistics and descriptive linguistics, theoretical linguistics and applied linguistics. And then list its main branches.

General linguistics deals with language, aiming at developing a theory that describe the rules of human language in general. Descriptive linguistics is the study of particular languages, attempting to build models that describe the rules of individual languages like Chinese and English.

"Theoretical linguistics studies language and languages with a view to constructing a theory of their structure and functions and without regard to any practical applications that the investigation of language and languages might have, whereas applied linguistics has as its concerns the application of the concepts and findings of linguistics to a variety of practical tasks, including language–teaching. ⋯ the goal of theoretical linguistics is the formulation of a satisfactory theory of the structure of language in general" (Lyons, 1981: 35).

As language is of different levels such as sound, form, and meaning, general linguistics can be divided into the following branches: phonetics, phonology, morphology, syntax, semantics, and pragmatics. These areas form the core of linguistics. In contrast with the core of linguistics, there are branches with interdisciplinary and applied orientation, such as psycholinguistics, cognitive linguistics, sociolinguistics, stylistics, anthropological linguistics, computational linguistics, applied linguistics, forensic linguistics, and so on. These are branches of macrolinguistics.

1.3.2 Traditional Study of Language in China

中国对于语言的传统研究可以追溯到春秋战国时期百家争鸣的名实之辩。对于意义的研究，西汉时有《尔雅》和扬雄的《方言》，东汉时有许慎的《说文解字》和刘熙的《释名》。对于汉语音韵研究，代表作有隋代的《切韵》、唐代的《唐韵》、宋代的《广韵》、金代的《五音集韵》、元代的《古今韵会举要》等（高天如，1989）。《马氏文通》（马建忠，1898）是中国关于汉语语法的第一部系统性著作。该书以古汉语为研究对象，把西方的语法学成功地引进中国，创立了第一个完整的汉语语法体系，奠定了中国现代语言学的第一块基石（戚雨村，1992）。

《荀子·正名》："后王之成名：刑名从商，爵名从周，文名从《礼》。散名之加于万物者，则从诸夏之成俗曲期，远方异俗之乡则因之而为通。""正利而为谓之事。正义而为谓之行。所以知之在人者谓之知。知有所合谓之智。""名无固宜，约之以命。约定俗成谓之宜，异于约则谓之不宜。"

《尔雅》是中国第一部词典，收录4300多个词语，按义类编排，计2091个条目，旨在提供语音、词汇和语法等方面都合乎规范的标准语。《尔雅》被认为是中国训诂的开山之作，是我国第一部按义类编排的综合性辞书，这些条目按类别分为"释诂"、"释言"、"释训"、"释亲"、"释宫"、"释器"、"释乐"、"释天"、"释地"、"释丘""释山"、"释水"、"释草"、"释木"、"释虫""释鱼"、"释鸟"、"释兽"、"释畜"等 19 篇。

　　谓女子，先生为姊，后生为妹。——《尔雅·释亲》

　　春为发生，夏为长赢，秋为收成，冬为安宁。——《尔雅·释天》

　　比翼双飞："南方有比翼鸟焉，不比不飞，其名谓之鹣鹣。"——《尔雅·释地》（https://www.guoxuebaike.cn/20210415/erya/ ）

　　《说文解字》是许慎在前人对汉字的研究基础上，创立 540 个部首，收录 9353 个汉字。它系统地阐述了汉字的造字规律——六书："周礼八岁入小学，保氏教国子先以六书。一曰指事，指事者视而可识，察而见意，上下是也。二曰象形，象形者画成其物，随体诘诎，日月是也。三曰形声，形声者以事为名，取譬相成，江河是也。四曰会意，会意者，比类合谊，以见指撝，武信是也。五曰转注，转注者建类一首，同意相受，考老是也。六曰假借，假借者本无其字，依声托事，令长是也。"许慎的解说，是历史上首次对六书定义的正式记载，后人多以此为依据。

1.3.3 Saussure as the Father of Modern Linguistics

The publication of Ferdinand de Saussure's *Course in General Linguistics* in 1916 was the starting point of structural linguistics, which presented a systematic study of language as an independent discipline. Thus, Saussure is regarded as the father of modern linguistics. His main contribution to structuralism is his concept of dichotomy in the study of language:

Synchronic and Diachronic Linguistics

Diachronic linguistics is the study of a language through the course of its history. A synchronic description takes a fixed instant (usually, but not necessarily, the present) as its point of observation. Most grammars are of this kind. Modern linguistics takes a priority of synchronic study.

Langue and Parole

Saussure distinguishes the linguistic competence of the speaker (the abstract linguistic system shared by all members of a speech community) as langue, and the actual phenomena or data of linguistics (utterances) as parole. This distinction takes a sociological point of view on language: langue exists in a collectivity; parole is uttered by individuals. Langue as conventions is relatively stable and systematic, parole as concrete utterances is subject to personal and situational constraints. For Saussure, parole is a mass of confused facts, thus not suitable for systematic investigation. What a linguist ought to do is to abstract langue from instances of parole, i.e., to discover the regularities governing all instances of parole and make them the subject of linguistics.

Signifier and Signified

In Saussure's view, language is a system of signs, each of which consists of two parts: SIGNIFIER (sound image/ symbol) and SIGNIFIED (concept). And the relationship between these two parts is arbitrary. We can only find the value of a sign from its relation to others, its position in the system. The two principal relations are SYNTAGMATIC and PARADIGMATIC relations.

Syntagmatic and Associative (Paradigmatic) Relations

Syntagmatic relation is a relation between one item and others in a sequence, or between elements which are all present, such as the relation between *weather* and the others in the sentence: *If the weather is nice, we'll go out*. There are syntactic and semantic conditions the words in a syntagmatic relation must meet. The associative relation refers to classes or sets of words substitutable for each other grammatically in sentences with the same structure. Words in an associative relation are comparable only in terms of syntax. Semantic factors are not taken into consideration here.

1.3.4 American Structuralism

American Structuralism is a branch of synchronic linguistics that emerged in the United States in the early 20th century, with representative figures – F. Boas (1858–1942), E. Sapir (1884–1939), B. L. Whorf (1897–1941), and Bloomfield (1887–1949). The pioneer scholars, including Boas, Sapir and Whorf, were all anthropologists who took interest in the indigenous languages of the American Indians and felt the urgent need to record these dying languages. Boas organized a survey of the indigenous languages of America north of Mexico; and contributed writing to the summary book *Handbook of American Indian Languages* (1911). His writing is a good summary of the descriptive approach to language.

Bloomfield is a landmark figure in American Structuralism that the period between 1933 and 1950 is known as Bloomfieldian Era. American descriptive linguistics reached its prime with the publication of Bloomfield's *Language* in 1933. Bloomfield's approach to linguistics is characterized by its emphasis on the scientific basis of linguistics and emphasis on formal procedures for the analysis of linguistic data. His IC (Immediate Constituents) analysis of a syntactic construction demonstrates the linearity and hierarchy of language. His behaviorist psychology to linguistics demonstrates its empirical philosophy and has significant influence on language teaching. The influence of Bloomfieldian structural linguistics declined in the late 1950s and early 1960s as the theory of generative grammar developed by Noam Chomsky came to predominate.

1.3.5 Generative Linguistics/ Transformational-Generative Grammar

The publication of Noam Chomsky's *Syntactic Structure* in 1957 marked the beginning of TG (Transformational-Generative) grammar. Chomsky proposed TG grammar to challenge the limitations of structuralist linguistics in America, and it turned to be a milestone in modern linguistics. TG grammar comprises phrase structure grammar and transformational grammar, through which language develops from basic deep structures to innumerous surface structures. It indeed solves the problem that IC analysis cannot explain, like difference between *John is easy to please.* and *John is eager to please.* The basic tenets of Chomsky's TG grammar include the dichotomy between competence and performance, universal grammar, deep structure and surface structure, and transformational rules. He attempts to establish principles of grammar shared by all languages, that is the universal grammar. This idea has influenced psychology, language teaching, computer science, and AI.

Competence and Performance

For Chomsky, competence is a language user's underlying knowledge about the system of rules. Performance refers to the actual use of language in concrete situations (Chomsky, 1965: 3). Competence enables a speaker to produce and understand an infinite number of sentences and to recognize grammatical mistakes and ambiguities. A speaker's competence is stable but his performance is often influenced by psychological and social factors. For example, a certain speaker's competence is stable but on certain occasions he may not perform very well due to various factors such as pressure, distress, anxiety, or embarrassment. Slips of tongue, false starts, unnecessary pause all belong to the imperfection of performance. A speaker may make grammatical mistakes in speech, but that does not mean he does not know the rule. A speaker's performance does not always match his competence.

Chomsky points out that this distinction is related to the langue–parole distinction of Saussure; but he does not accept the view of seeing langue as a mere systematic inventory of items. Saussure takes a sociological view of language and his notion of langue is a matter of social conventions, while

Chomsky looks at language from a psychological point of view and considers linguistic competence as a property of the mind of a speaker.

1.3.6 Functional Linguistics

In contrast with formal linguistics which sees language form determines meaning; functional linguistics states that our communicative meaning determines our choice of language forms. Functional linguistics originates in Europe, comprising of several famous linguistic schools.

The first famous functional linguistic school is the Prague School centered in Prague with Nikolais Trubetzkoy(1890–1938), Roman Jakobson (1896–1982) and V. Mathesius(1882–1945) as leading figures. Its most important contributions are: first, synchronic study of language is fully justified. Second, there is an emphasis on the systemic character of language. Language elements are held to be in functional contrast or opposition. Third, Trubetzkoy gives an accurate definition of phoneme, and makes a distinction between phonetics and phonology. Fourth, a stress on the study of function of language is made, such as Roman Jakobson. Fifth, Mathesius' functional sentence perspective of THEME and RHEME gives a perspective to describe how information is distributed in sentences.

The London School is represented by B. Malinowsky (1884–1942), J. R. Firth (1890–1960) and M. A. K. Halliday (1925–2018). As an anthropologist, Malinowsky observed languages in primitive communities and underlined the importance of context of situation in understanding verbal meaning. He saw language as a mode of action and coined the term Phatic Communion. Firth was the first Professor of General Linguistics in Britain in 1944, and he was influenced by Saussure and Malinowsky. Firth saw language as a social process and furthered the study of context. He classified context into situational and linguistic ones. Halliday was Firth's student and the founder of Systemic-Functional (SF) Grammar. For SF Grammar, it is social function of language that helps language users to make a choice from the system of meaning potentials. Halliday learned Chinese language for his BA and MA. His doctoral dissertation was titled "The Language of the Chinese 'Secret History of the Mongols' " under the supervision of Firth. Thus, SF grammar can be applied in analyzing Chinese.

Further Readings:

Jakobson, R. 1960. *"Linguistics and Poetry"* in *Style and Language*, ed. Sebeok, T.A. Cambridge Mass: MIT Press.

Lyons, John. 1981. *Language and Linguistics*. Cambridge: Cambridge University Press.

Widdowson, H. G. 2000. *Linguistics*. Shanghai: Shanghai Foreign Languages Education Press.

Yule, G. 2000. *The Study of Language.* Beijing: Foreign Language Teaching and Research Press.

许慎, 2012.《说文解字》, 北京：中华书局.

荀况, 2011.《荀子》, 北京：中华书局.

Questions and Exercises:

1. Define the following terms:

language, design features of language, functions of language, linguistics and its research principles, major distinctions in linguistics.

2. Find more examples to illustrate design features of language, and functions of language.

3. Why is Saussure seen as the father of modern linguistics?

4. What are the differences between modern linguistics and traditional grammar?

5. What are the differences between competence and performance? What's the relationship between this dichotomy and Saussure's distinction between Lange and Parole?

6. Read the classic works of traditional study of Chinese and make your comment concerning Chinese language and humanity.

Chapter 2

Phonetics and Phonology: The Sounds and Sound Patterns of Language

语 言 学 导 论
新文科思政教程

2.1 Introduction

Speaking is the primary mode of language, and then is its written mode. To learn how speech sounds are produced and classified can help us pronounce properly and speak fluently. It also helps us get an answer to such questions like "why I can't pronounce [l] in 老师 ?" asked by a student from Hunan Province.

In learning a foreign language, we encounter pronunciation difficulties. Why foreigners always say Chinese without tones, like "你 吃 了 吗 ?" Why Chinese students find some sounds difficult to pronounce in learning English, like [θ, ð]; and [ʁ] difficult to pronounce in learning French words like *au revoir*. Besides learning how to produce speech sounds, we also need to learn the sound pattern of English, that is English phonology, especially in contrast with Chinese phonology to better facilitate our master of these two languages. Many pronunciation difficulties will be solved in this chapter.

Learning Objectives:

1. Remember the following terms: (articulatory) phonetics, phonology, International Phonetic Alphabet, consonant, vowel, cardinal vowels, broad and narrow transcription, minimal pair, phoneme, allophone, complementary distribution, syllable, Maximal Onset Principle

2.Understand: the difference of sound patterns between Chinese and English

3.Illustrate with examples: Can describe the main consonants in E; Can use narrow transcription to describe the actual pronunciation of words

4.Tell stories: typical features of Chinese dialects

Lead-in Questions:

1.Read the Chinese tongue twister *牛郎恋刘娘* . Tell stories about special features of Chinese dialects.

牛郎恋刘娘，刘娘念牛郎。牛郎连连恋刘娘，刘娘连连恋牛郎。牛郎年年念刘娘，刘娘年年念牛郎。郎恋娘来娘恋郎，念娘恋娘念郎恋郎。牛恋刘来刘恋牛，刘念牛来牛念刘。郎恋娘来娘恋郎，娘念郎来郎念娘。

2.Watch the film *My Fair Lady*, and find the pronunciation difference between different social classes in Britain. Find more examples about special pronunciations of English dialects.

2.2 Phonetics

Human beings are capable of producing various sounds of which only some are chosen as sounds in our languages. Different languages have different choices of sounds. That is the reason why we Chinese find it difficult to pronounce [θ, ð] in English, and [ʁ] in French words like *au revoir*. There may be sounds more difficult to pronounce in Arabic and African languages. The reason is the fact that Chinese language does not have such sounds, and thus native Chinese speakers are not used to making such sounds.

There are two main subfields concerning the study of speech sounds. Phonetics studies the physical facts of speech sounds. It studies how speech sounds are produced, transmitted, and perceived. It is concerned with all the sounds that occur in the world's languages. It is divided into three areas: Articulatory Phonetics is the study of the production of speech sounds. Perceptual or Auditory Phonetics is concerned with the perception of speech sounds. Acoustic Phonetics is the study of the physical properties of speech sounds.

In contrast, Phonology studies the structure and systematic patterning of sound in a language. It aims to "discover the principles that govern the way sounds are organized in languages, and to explain the variations that occur"(Crystal, 1997: 162).

2.2.1 Speech Organs

Speech organs are those parts of our body involved in the production of speech sounds. The speech organs consist of 3 major areas: the pharyngeal cavity, the oral cavity and the nasal cavity. In making speech sounds, our lungs work as the power engine. The air goes from our lungs, through the trachea, to the vocal folds in the center of our larynx. From the vocal folds upwards, the air is modified at different position in the cavities in various ways, making different kinds of speech sounds. When the vocal folds are spread apart, the air from the lungs passes without any restriction. Speech sounds thus produced are described as voiceless. Consonants [p, t, f] are produced in this way. When the vocal folds are close together, the air from the lungs has to break through them, making the vocal folds vibrating against each other. Speech sounds produced in this way are described as voiced. Consonants [b, d, v] and vowels are produced in this way. And when the vocal folds are totally closed, no air can pass through them. The result of such a gesture is the glottal stop [ʔ], such as in American English word *button*. We can easily distinguish voiceless and voiced sounds by placing our fingertips gently on the front part of our larynx – our "Adam's Apple". We can feel no vibration when producing consonants [p, t, f], but feel vibration in producing consonants [b, d, v] and vowels.

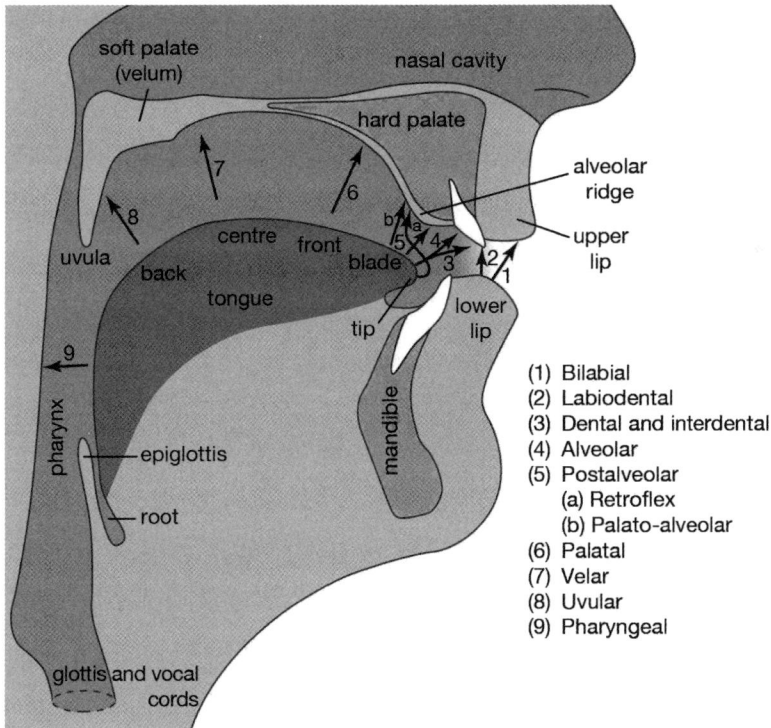

Figure 2.1 Speech Organs

https://www.britannica.com/science/phonetics

The distinction between consonants and vowels lies in the obstruction of airstream. Consonants are made "by a closure in the vocal tract, or by a narrowing which is so marked that air cannot escape without producing audible friction." In contrast, a vowel is produced without such a "stricture" so that "air escapes in a relatively unimpeded way through the mouth or nose" (Crystal, 1997:154).

2.2.2 The IPA

The IPA can refer either to the International Phonetic Association or to the International Phonetic Alphabet. The International Phonetic Alphabet is the association's alphabet, published periodically in chart form since 1888, usually referred to as the chart of the IPA. The chart has been refined and updated over the years to accommodate the need to represent symbolically the sounds of the world's languages. The purpose of the association and of its alphabet has been to devise and promulgate a uniform standard for phonetic writing, known commonly as phonetic transcription.

The International Phonetic Association as an association was established in Paris in 1886 by French and British language teachers led by Paul Passy (a French linguist, founder of the International Phonetic Association). The association was originally named the Phonetic Teachers' Association, and in 1897 it became the International Phonetic Association (IPA).

Otto Jespersen was the first to propose the idea of establishing a phonetic alphabet. In 1886 Otto Jespersen joined the Phonetic Teachers' Association and met Passy, with whom he had only corresponded previously. In August 1888,

THE INTERNATIONAL PHONETIC ALPHABET (revised to 2020)

CONSONANTS (PULMONIC)

© ① ⑤ 2020 IPA

	Bilabial	Labiodental	Dental	Alveolar	Postalveolar	Retroflex	Palatal	Velar	Uvular	Pharyngeal	Glottal
Plosive	p b			t d		ʈ ɖ	c ɟ	k ɡ	q ɢ		ʔ
Nasal	m	ɱ		n		ɳ	ɲ	ŋ	N		
Trill	ʙ			r					R		
Tap or Flap		ⱱ		ɾ		ɽ					
Fricative	ɸ β	f v	θ ð	s z	ʃ ʒ	ʂ ʐ	ç ʝ	x ɣ	χ ʁ	ħ ʕ	h ɦ
Lateral fricative				ɬ ɮ							
Approximant		ʋ		ɹ		ɻ	j	ɰ			
Lateral approximant				l		ɭ	ʎ	ʟ			

Symbols to the right in a cell are voiced, to the left are voiceless. Shaded areas denote articulations judged impossible.

CONSONANTS (NON-PULMONIC)

Clicks	Voiced implosives	Ejectives
ʘ Bilabial	ɓ Bilabial	ʼ Examples:
ǀ Dental	ɗ Dental/alveolar	pʼ Bilabial
ǃ (Post)alveolar	ʄ Palatal	tʼ Dental/alveolar
ǂ Palatoalveolar	ɠ Velar	kʼ Velar
ǁ Alveolar lateral	ʛ Uvular	sʼ Alveolar fricative

OTHER SYMBOLS

ʍ Voiceless labial-velar fricative

w Voiced labial-velar approximant

ɥ Voiced labial-palatal approximant

ʜ Voiceless epiglottal fricative

ʢ Voiced epiglottal fricative

ʡ Epiglottal plosive

ɕ ʑ Alveolo-palatal fricatives

ɺ Voiced alveolar lateral flap

ɧ Simultaneous ʃ and x

Affricates and double articulations can be represented by two symbols joined by a tie bar if necessary.

t͡s k͡p

VOWELS

Where symbols appear in pairs, the one to the right represents a rounded vowel.

SUPRASEGMENTALS

ˈ	Primary stress	ˌfoʊnəˈtɪʃən
ˌ	Secondary stress	
ː	Long	eː
ˑ	Half-long	eˑ
̆	Extra-short	ĕ
ǀ	Minor (foot) group	
ǁ	Major (intonation) group	
.	Syllable break	ɹi.ækt
‿	Linking (absence of a break)	

DIACRITICS

̥	Voiceless	n̥ d̥	̤	Breathy voiced	b̤ a̤	̪	Dental	t̪ d̪
̬	Voiced	s̬ t̬	̰	Creaky voiced	b̰ a̰	̺	Apical	t̺ d̺
ʰ	Aspirated	tʰ dʰ	̼	Linguolabial	t̼ d̼	̻	Laminal	t̻ d̻
̹	More rounded	ɔ̹	ʷ	Labialized	tʷ dʷ	̃	Nasalized	ẽ
̜	Less rounded	ɔ̜	ʲ	Palatalized	tʲ dʲ	ⁿ	Nasal release	dⁿ
̟	Advanced	u̟	ˠ	Velarized	tˠ dˠ	ˡ	Lateral release	dˡ
̠	Retracted	e̠	ˤ	Pharyngealized	tˤ dˤ	̚	No audible release	d̚
̈	Centralized	ë	̴	Velarized or pharyngealized	ɫ			
̽	Mid-centralized	ẽ	̝	Raised	e̝ (ɹ̝ = voiced alveolar fricative)			
̩	Syllabic	n̩	̞	Lowered	e̞ (β̞ = voiced bilabial approximant)			
̯	Non-syllabic	e̯	̘	Advanced Tongue Root	e̘			
˞	Rhoticity	ɚ ɚ˞	̙	Retracted Tongue Root	e̙			

TONES AND WORD ACCENTS

LEVEL			CONTOUR		
e̋ or	ꜛ	Extra high	ě or	꜠	Rising
é	ꜛ	High	ê	꜡	Falling
ē	ꜛ	Mid	e᷄	꜠	High rising
è	ꜛ	Low	e᷅	꜠	Low rising
ȅ	ꜛ	Extra low	e᷈	Ꜣ	Rising-falling
ꜜ	Downstep		ꜛ		Global rise
ꜛ	Upstep		ꜜ		Global fall

Some diacritics may be placed above a symbol with a descender, e.g. ŋ̊ the Phonetic Teachers' Association published a standardized alphabet intended for transcription of multiple languages, reflecting its members' consensus that only one set of alphabets ought to be used for all languages. it has been revised from time to time to include new discoveries and changes in phonetic theory and practice. The latest version has been revised in 2020.

The general principle of the IPA is to provide one letter for each distinctive sound (speech segment), and the same symbol should be used for that sound in any language in which it appears. The IPA is based on the Latin script, and uses as few non−Latin Letters as possible, using new letters and diacritics only when absolutely necessary.

2.2.3 Consonants

Consonants are made with an obstruction of airstream in the vocal tract. The stricture is made by at least two articulators. So, consonants can be described according to their place of articulation and manner of articulation. In other words, where the airstream is modified and how it is modified.

2.2.3.1 Manner of Articulation

Concerning the manner of articulation, consonants are described according to how the airstream is modified. The following are the major categories of consonants with the 24 English consonants as examples.

1) Stops (or explosives): A stop is made by a brief complete closure of the articulators so that the airstream stops and then passes abruptly. In English, [p, b, t, d, k, g] are stops.

2) Nasals (or nasal stops): A nasal is made by blocking the airstream from the oral cavity and letting it go through the nasal cavity. In English, [m, n, ŋ] are nasals.

3) Fricatives: A fricative is made by close approximation of two articulators so that the airstream is partially obstructed and a "fricative" sound is made. In English, [f, v, θ, ð, s, z, ʃ, ʒ] are fricatives.

4) Affricates: An affricate is made by combining a stop followed immediately afterwards by a fricative at the same place of articulation. In English, [tʃ, dʒ] are affricates.

5) Approximants (or semi-vowels): An approximant is made by the articulators approaching each other but not narrowly enough to cause audible friction. In English, [w, y] are approximants. The sound [h], as in *hello*, can also be classified as an approximant because of the way it combines with other sounds.

6) Liquids: A liquid is made with a minimal constriction allowing airstream to pass freely. Liquids consist of a lateral approximant [l], with airstream flowing around the sides of the tongue; and [r] with airstream flowing through the center of the mouth.

2.2.3.2 Place of Articulation

Place of articulation refers to the point where a consonant is made. When airstream passes through the vocal folds, a consonant may be produced at any place between the lips and the vocal folds. The following are terms used to describe consonants in terms of where they are articulated with the 24 English consonants as examples. Besides, consonants can be voiced or voiceless according to whether the vocal folds vibrate or not.

1) Bilabials: A bilabial consonant is made with the two lips. In English, [p, b, m, w] are bilabials. Only [p] is voiceless, and the other three are voiced.

2) Labio-dentals: A labio-dental is made with the lower lip and upper teeth. In English, [f, v] are labio-dentals.

3) Dentals: A dental is made with the tongue tip or blade between the teeth, or just behind the upper teeth. In English, [θ, ð] are dentals.

4) Alveolars: An alveolar is made with the tongue tip at the alveolar ridge, behind the teeth. In English, [t, d, s, z, n, l, r] are alveolars, of which [t, s] are voiceless and the others voiced.

5) Retroflexes: A retroflex is made with the tongue tip or blade retroflexed (curled back) so that the underside of the tongue tip or blade forms a stricture with the back of the alveolar ridge or the hard palate. In Chinese Putonghua, the retroflex fricative [ʂ] is typical as in 书 [ʂu], 事儿 [ʂɚ]. The Chinese words 字儿，刺儿 are also retroflexes.

6) Palatals: A palatal is made with the front or body of the tongue raised to the palatal region. In English, [ʃ, ʒ, tʃ, dʒ, j] are palatals, of which [ʃ, tʃ] are voiceless and the other three are voiced. In some systems, [ʃ, ʒ] are also known as postalveolars.

7) Velars: A velar is made with the back of the tongue raised to the soft palate (also called velum). In English, [k, g, ŋ] are velars, of which [k] is voiceless and the other two voiced.

8) Uvulars: A uvular is made with the back of the tongue raised

against or near the uvular, that is further back in the mouth than velar consonants. In French, [ʁ] is a uvular as in revoir.

9) Glottal: In English, there is only one glottal approximant [h], which is made with the glottis (the space between the vocal folds) open.

Manner of Articulation	Place of Articulation						
	Bilabial	Labiodental	Dental	Alveolar	Palatal	Velar	Glottal
Stop/ Plosive	p, b			t, d		k, g	
Nasal	m			n		ŋ	
Fricative		f, v	θ, ð	s, z	ʃ, ʒ		
Approximant	w			r	j		h
Lateral				l			
Affricate					tʃ, dʒ		

Table 2.1 A Chart of English Consonants

The consonants of English can be described in the following manner: Voicing +Place +Manner of Articulation, for example:

[p]: voiceless bilabial stop

[z]: voiced alveolar fricative

[n]: voiced alveolar nasal

[h]: voiceless glottal approximant

2.2.4 Vowels

Cardinal vowels, as exhibited by the vowel diagram in the IPA chart, are a set of vowel qualities arbitrarily defined, fixed and unchanging, intended to provide a frame of reference for describing the actual vowels of existing languages. The current "cardinal vowels" system was systematized by Daniel Jones (British) in a number of writings from 1917 onwards, particularly in his *An Outline of English Phonetics* (1962).

A vowel sound whose quality does not change over the duration of the vowel is called a pure vowel or a monophthong. In contrast a diphthong (or a vowel glide) is a combination of two adjacent vowel sounds within the same syllable. The tongue moves during the pronunciation of the vowel. If a single movement of the tongue is involved, the glides are called diphthongs. English has 8 diphthongs: [ei], [ai], [au], [ɔi], [əu], [iə], [uə], [eə]. A double movement produces a triphthong. They are really diphthongs followed by the schwa 中性元音 [ə], found in English words like *player* [pleiə] and *flower* [flauə].

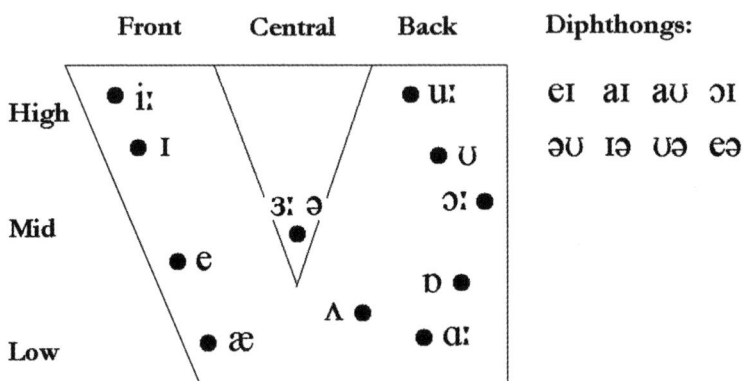

Table 2.2 English Vowels

Because vowels are made without audible friction, the description of vowels are different from consonants. "To describe vowel sounds, we must consider the ways in which the tongue influences the 'shape' through which the airflow must pass" (Yule, 2006: 38). There are four criteria to describe a vowel:

1)the height of the tongue (high, mid, low);

2)the position of the highest part of the tongue (front, central, back);

3)the length or tenseness of the vowel (tense, lax);

4)the degree of lip-rounding (rounded, unrounded).

In English, there are 12 monophthongs, of which four front vowels: [i:], [i], [e], [æ]; two central vowels: [ə:], [ə]; and six back vowels: [u:], [u], [ɔ:], [ɔ], [ʌ], [a:].

We can now describe the English vowels in this way:

[i:] high front tense unrounded vowel

[ʊ] high back lax rounded vowel

[ə] mid central lax unrounded vowel

[ɒ] low back lax rounded vowel

2.2.5 Traditional Study of Speech Sounds in China

《汉语拼音方案》*Scheme for the Chinese Phonetic Alphabet*

《汉语拼音方案》是在 20 世纪 50 年代制订出来的。新中国成立以后，中国文字改革委员会普遍征求和广泛收集各方面对拼音方案的意见，进行分析和研究，于 1956 年 2 月拟订出《汉语拼音方案（草案）》。这个方案经审议和多次修订，报请国务院全体会议通过，最后在 1958 年 2 月由第一届全国人民代表大会第五次会议批准作为正式方案推行。汉语拼音方案是在过去各种注音法的基础上发展起来的，可以说是我国人民创制各种汉语注音法的经验总结。

汉字不是拼音文字，为了标记汉字的读音，人们曾采用直音法、反切法或注音字母（注音符号）。但这些注音法都有缺点。前两种要以认识大量汉字为基础，如果没有音同或音近的字就难以注音。注音符号曾起过一定作用，但它不完全是音素字母，注音不够准确，书写也不够方便。《汉语拼音方案》基本上克服了上述缺点，能够准确给汉字注音。它采用国际上流行的拉丁字母，既容易为广大群众掌握，又便于国际间的文化交流。

古代汉语的语音和反切

中古汉语的语音，以《切韵》系统为标准。《切韵》是隋代陆法言所著韵书。书成于隋文帝仁寿元年（601）。唐代初年被定为官韵。增订本甚多。《切韵》原书已失传，其所反映的语音系统因《广韵》等增订本而得以完整地流传下来。《切韵》的系统并不能代表当时（隋代）的首都（长安）的实际语音，它只代表一种被认为文学语言的语音系统。这种语音系统纯然是属于书面语言的；从唐代到清代，一直是基本上遵守着这一个语音标准，例如律诗就必须依照这一个语音系统来押韵，否则被认为不合格。固然，律诗用韵比《切韵》的韵部要宽些，但那只是范围大小的问题，从整个系统来看，还是大致不乱的。

这个系统是参照了古音和方言来规定的。依古音应该分别的音，就给它们分别开来，哪一种方言能照古音系统读出一个分别来，就给它们分别开来，哪一种方言能照古音系统读出一个分别来，它就算是合于规范。这个规范虽然是人为的，却不是没有依据的。曾经有些学者希望人们依照这个规范来发音，这个空想没有能够实现，但是这个语音系统被公认为文学语言的语音规范，则是没有疑问的。

《切韵》的语音系统，可以从两方面观察出来：第一是反切，第二是韵目。一般所谓《切韵》系统也就是《广韵》的系统。这里的反切和韵目也就是《广韵》的反切和韵目。

反切是中国古代的拼音法，例如"东，德红切"，这就表示"东"字的读音是由"德"和"红"拼成的。实际上，反切上字（德）只取声母（t），反切下字（红）只取韵母（uŋ），得到"东"（tuŋ）。"东"和"德"同声母，是双声；"东"和"红"同韵母，是叠韵。我们只要看《广韵》里的双声字有几类，就知道《切韵》系统里有多少声母；再看《广韵》里的叠韵字有几类，就知道《切韵》系统里有多少韵母。《广韵》共有 35 个声母，分为喉音（如"晓、匣"）、牙音（如"见、溪、群、疑"）、舌音（如"端、透、定、泥、来、娘"）、齿音（如"精、清、从、心"）和唇音（如"帮、滂、并、明"）。古代声母分清音和浊音，如"精"为全清，"清"为次清，"群、定、匣、从、并"为全浊，"疑、泥、娘、明"为次浊。<u>《广韵》共有 206 个韵，但如果除了声调的分别不算，就只有 61 个韵类，141 个韵母</u>。因为《切韵》系统不代表一时一地的语音，那么 61 个韵类和 141 个韵母就不能理解为同时存在的。例如支脂之是三个韵，是因为从历史来源说它们是有分别的，这种分别也许还在方言里留下痕迹，但并不意味着当时的长安话里能区别这三个韵。不过我们承认 206 韵的系统是有好处的，因为由此可以上推古，下推现代方言（王，2015：49-54）。

汉字的发音是变化发展的。根据清代学者顾炎武等人研究的结果，《诗经》里每字都有固定的读音，不过先秦的字音另是一个系统，和后代的读音系统不同。如果按照先秦的语音系统来读《诗经》，每一个韵脚都自然谐和。段玉裁等人发现谐声偏旁和《诗经》韵脚的一致性。段玉裁说"同声必同部"，意思是说，凡同一谐声偏旁的字，一定同属一个韵部，也一定和《诗经》的韵脚相符，因为先秦的韵部是由《诗经》的韵脚概括出来的（王，2015: 60）。关于《诗经》的读音及变化可以参看王力的《汉语语音史》（王，2010）。以下三例以窥汉字读音的变化与古诗的押韵：

1）南北朝时期北朝民歌《敕勒歌》："敕勒川，阴山下。天似穹庐，笼盖四野。天苍苍，野茫茫。风吹草低见牛羊。""苍、茫、羊"直到今天，用所有的方言去读，都是押韵的。可是前面"下、野"处在非押韵不可的位置上，难道它们不押韵吗？不是的，"下、野"直到宋代以前，人们读起来都会感觉到押韵，北宋时朝廷编了一部按韵编排的字书《广韵》，"下、野"都是《广韵》马韵字，既然同属马韵，也就说明它们是互相押韵的字。今天的南昌、梅州、厦门、潮州、福州、建瓯等地方言，"下、野"读起来也还是押韵的。为什么全国大部分方言都读得押不上韵？结论只有一个："下、野"的读音古今发生了变化。

2）贺知章的《回乡偶书》其一："少小离家老大回，乡音无改鬓毛衰。儿童相见不相识，笑问客从何处来。"这是一首七绝，按要求，"回、衰、来"处在押韵的位置上。李军（2020）指出，贺知章《回乡偶书》的押韵和"衰"的音义争议主要分歧在于"衰"字取音与取义不合。其实，在押韵上，"衰"只能读 cuī，灰韵，非脂、支韵，更非出韵，因为韵脚字"回、衰、来"中的"回""来"已经是"灰""哈"同用，这说明贺知章掌握并严格遵循近体诗"灰""哈"同用的押韵规定；在词义上，"衰"与"榱、蓑、缞"等为同源关系，词源义为"下垂"，可引申出"差等"等义，由"递减"义可再引申出事物发展由盛而衰的"衰落、衰退"等义，以及事物数量由多而少的"稀疏、稀少"等义，其所指之物颜色相同或相近：黄（白）或白，所以"鬓毛衰"字面释义为"鬓发又少又白",这合乎"鬓毛衰"的言外之意"衰老"。而且用"衰"此义的古诗也很多,如陆游《感怀》"老抱遗书隐故山,镜中衰鬓似霜菅",卢照邻《送幽州陈参军赴任寄呈乡曲父老》"红颜如昨日,衰鬓似秋天"等,其中"衰"可释为"变白"。这可为解决"衰"字在辞书、作品选、语文教学中的"押韵""释义"分歧提供参考意见。

3)白居易的《琵琶行》,开头有"浔阳江头夜送客,枫叶荻花秋瑟瑟","客、瑟"处在押韵的位置上。宋代以来,《琵琶行》的"瑟瑟",又有"索索(槭槭、摵摵)"的异文,"索索"和"槭槭、摵摵"记录的是同一个词。这说明《琵琶行》早期的本子并没有定作"瑟瑟",理论上,白居易原诗可能作"瑟瑟",也可能作"索索(槭槭、摵摵)",不可能既作"瑟瑟",又作"索索(槭槭、摵摵)"。我们不能不加论证,武断地选择"瑟瑟",那种做法没有根据,是不科学的。经过研究,"瑟"和"客"在唐代韵腹和韵尾都相差很远,不能押韵;"索索(槭槭、摵摵)"跟"客"韵腹和韵尾相同,可以押韵。可见,白居易原诗有可能是"索索(槭槭、摵摵)",作"瑟瑟"是后人而改。没有唐代语音方面的知识,就无法对异文做出正确而必要的选择,只能想当然耳。

2.3 Phonology

Phonetics is concerned with the physical facts of speech sounds; and phonology is concerned with the social conventions of a language. Phonology studies the structure and systematic patterning of sound in a language. It tells us the different rules of sound arrangement between Chinese and English.

2.3.1 Phoneme

In learning English pronunciation, Chinese students may find difficulties in making the speech sounds [θ, ð], such as to distinguish *mouth* and *mouse, thin* and *sin, think* and *sink, breathe* and *breeze, then* and *Zen, scythe* and *size*. This is due to a fact that [θ, ð] do not exist in Chinese language, and it takes time to learn. Some Chinese students may also find it difficult to distinguish sounds [w] and [v] in English, for example in words *wine* and *vine, west and vest, verse* and *worse, veil* and *whale*. The reason for this is that there is no distinction between [w] and [v] in Chinese Putonghua, we can say [ˈwei ʃən mə] or [ˈvei ʃən mə] (为什么).

From the above examples, we see that Chinese and English have different choices of speech sounds in each language system. And each chosen speech sound has the power to distinguish two words in the language.

According to Aitchison (1992: 39), a phoneme is the smallest segment of sound which can distinguish two words. The two words in a language which differ from each other by only one distinctive sound and which also differ in meaning are called a minimal pair, such as *mouth* and *mouse, scythe* and *size, wine* and *vine*. Minimal pairs test can be used to find out which sound substitutions cause differences of meaning in a language. By convention, phonemic transcriptions are placed between slant lines (/ /) while phonetic transcriptions are placed between square brackets ([ ]). A phoneme is the smallest unit and functions contrastively in a language. There are 48 phonemes in English, of which 44 are seen as separate sound units and four (/ts, dz, tr, dr/) are seen as consonant clusters. A phoneme is an abstract unit and can be represented by different phones in different phonetic environments.

2.3.2 Allophone

The different phones which represent a phoneme in different phonetic environments are called allophones of that phoneme. For example, the phoneme /l/ in English is pronounced differently in different phonetic environments. It is clear [l] before a vowel; it is dark [ɫ] at the end of a syllable; and it is devoiced [l̥] when follows [p] or [k]. The allophones of the same phoneme are described in phonetic transcription with diacritics to show the minute differences of sound. This kind of phonetic transcription with diacritics to show more phonetic detail is called narrow transcription in contrast with broad transcription with only a simple set of symbols. These three phones are allophones of the phoneme /l/ in the three phonetic environments. They each occur in a different phonetic environment, and they together form the whole pronunciation condition of /l/ in English. This distribution of allophones of a phoneme is called complementary distribution.

/l/: [l] / _____ V
    [ɫ] / V _____
    [l̥]/ [p]/[k] _____

Table 2.3 Allophones of /l/   Table 2.4 Complementary Distribution

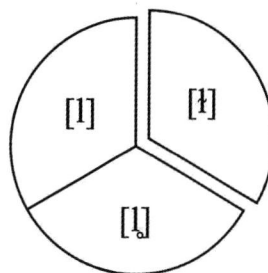

Besides the distribution rule of a phoneme, a phoneme may also have free variants. The different pronunciation may be caused by dialect or personal habit. Such a phenomenon is called free variation. For example, the difference between

British and American pronunciations, like words *either, direction, pass.*

"The crucial distinction between phonemes and allophones is that substituting one phoneme for another will result in a word with a different meaning (as well as a different pronunciation), but substituting allophones only results in a different (and perhaps unusual) pronunciation of the same word" (Yule, 2006: 45).

2.3.3 Suprasegmentals

Suprasegmental features are those phonemic features that involve more than one sound segment. An important suprasegmental unit is syllable, and major suprasegmental features include stress, tone and intonation.

2.3.3.1 Syllable

A syllable is a unit of organization for a sequence of speech sounds typically made up of a nucleus (most often a vowel) with optional initial and final margins (typically, consonants). Syllables are often considered the phonological "building blocks" of words (Kenneth, 2003: 254). Words with one syllable are monosyllabic, while words with more than one syllable are polysyllabic. Chinese language is monosyllabic.

The general structure of a syllable consists of three segments: onset, nucleus and coda. The latter two segments constitute the rhyme of a syllable. In most languages onsets are preferred yet optional — although they are required in some languages. The onset can be a consonant or a combination of more than one consonant (a consonant cluster). In fact, the nucleus is the only universally obligatory component of a syllable, which is often made by a vowel. Sometimes there are exceptions like *cotton* /kɔtn/ and *table* /teɪbl/, with syllabic consonants functioning as a nucleus. No language requires codas. In most languages codas are optional, and they are restricted or even prohibited in others. A syllable that has no coda is called an open syllable while a syllable with a coda is called a closed syllable.

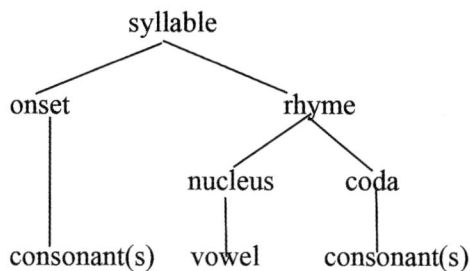

syllable

onset   rhyme

                nucleus   coda

consonant(s)   vowel   consonant(s)

Different languages have different sound combinations, for example, Chinese syllable stresses the onset and nucleus part while coda is restricted to consonants /n, ŋ/. For onset, Chinese syllable permits single consonant rather than consonant cluster. The Putonghua syllable is represented as (C) V (C). In contrast in English, both onset and coda can be empty or can consist of a consonant cluster. The onset can be filled by as many as three consonants and the coda by four consonants, such as *sixths* /sɪksθs/. Thus the English syllable may be represented as (((C) C) C) V ((((C) C) C) C). In English polysyllabic words, the division of syllables should be in accordance with Maximal Onset Principle, which states that when there is a choice as to where to place a consonant, it is put into the onset rather than the coda (Radford, et al., 2000: 91–92). For example, *telling* is pronounced as /teliŋ/.

Concerning the sequence of phonemes in a syllable or a word, there is a branch of phonology – Phonotactics that deals with restrictions in a language on the permissible combinations of phonemes. Phonotactics defines permissible syllable structure, consonant clusters and vowel sequences by means of phonotactic constraints. For example, we can use phonemes /k, b, l, i/ to form English words such as *blik, klib, bilk, kilb*. But our phonological knowledge forbids us from making words like *bkil, ilbk, ilkb, lbki* in English. These impossible sequences are called systematic gaps. In contrast, sequences that are possible but do not occur yet are called accidental gaps. When new words are coined, they may fill some accidental gaps but they will never fill systematic gaps. Also, if three consonants should cluster together at the beginning of a word, the combination should obey the following three rules: The first phoneme must be /s/; the second phoneme must be /p/ or /t/ or /k/ or /m/; and the third phoneme must be /l/ or /r/ or /w/ or /j/ (e.g. *skewer, scratch, spring, street, splash*).

2.3.3.2 Stress

Stress refers to the relative emphasis or prominence given to a certain syllable in a word or to a certain word in a phrase or sentence. The syllable is stressed through increased loudness and vowel length. In transcription, a raised vertical line [ˈ]is used before the syllable it relates to, and a secondary stress is marked with a lowered vertical line [ˌ], for example, *integration* [ˌɪntɪˈɡreɪʃn]. At the word level, stress only applies to words with at least two syllables. At the sentence level, stress runs over the word boundary. Native speakers only stress the most important content words in a sentence and allow the rest of the words to fall away unstressed.

At the word level, stress is placed on a different syllable for the different grammatical class a word plays. Phrase (or sentence) stress is used to provide emphasis on a certain element of a given point, wherein phonetic stress focuses the audience's attention on what is most important in the message. And stress also change over history and exhibit regional or dialectal differences.

2.3.3.3 Tone

Tone refers to the pitch and pitch changes in words of certain languages. Chinese is a tone language or tonal language, in which a syllable such as [ma] can have at least four meanings depending on the tone on which it is spoken: first tone ([ma1]), second tone ([ma2]), third tone ([ma3]), and fourth tone ([ma4]) (the transcription of the four tones is in accordance with *Scheme for the Chinese Phonetic Alphabet)* (Huang &Liao, 2002: 100). Actually, there are different characters with the same pronunciation and tone form, which constitute a total of about 22,700 single-character words in *Hanyu Da Cidian*, which has a large Chinese vocabulary of about 375,000 words (including single-character words, compound words, and idioms/ chengyu) (Luo, 1993). It is said that there are 6,000 to 9,000 common Chinese characters (Huang &Liao, 2002: 195).

The current four tones of Putonghua come from the tones of ancient Chinese (in the Northern and Southern Dynasties from 420 to 589). There are differences between tones of current Chinese dialects. Most Chinese dialects have four tones, while others have 3 to 10 tones (Huang &Liao, 2002: 78–87).

2.3.3.4 Intonation

Intonation involves the occurrence of recurring fall–rise tone patterns, each of which is used with a set of relatively constituent meanings, either on single words or on groups of words of varying length (Cruttenden, 1997: 7). The three major patterns of intonation in English are: falling intonation, rising intonation and fall–rise intonation. A falling intonation is very common in wh–questions. We also use falling intonation when we say something definite, or when we want to be very clear about something. Rising intonation is common in yes–no questions. We use fall–rise intonation at the end of statements when we want to say that we are not sure, or when we may have more to add.

For example:

Where's the nearest post-office?

I think we are completely lost.

It rained every day in the first week. (but things improved after that).

(https://dictionary.cambridge.org/zhs/%E8%AF%AD%E6%B3%95/%E8%8B%B1%E5%BC%8F%E8%AF%AD%E6%B3%95/intonation)

2.3.3.5 Chinese Syllable

汉语普通话音节由声母、韵母和声调组成。其中，韵母包括：韵头、和韵（韵腹、韵尾）。普通话的音节结构特点如下：

1. 一个音节最多可由四个音素符号（或六个汉语拼音字母）来拼写，如窗 [chuang1]（声母是 ch、韵头是 u、韵腹是 a、韵尾是 ng）。

2. 元音在音节中占优势。每个音节总要有元音，元音符号可以多至三个，并须连续出现，分别充当韵头、韵腹和韵尾，如桥 [qiao2]。

3. 音节可以没有辅音，如鹅 [e2]；没有两个辅音相连的音节，音节末辅音只限于 n 和 ng。

4. 汉语音节不能没有声调，不能没有韵腹（主要元音）；可以没有辅音声母、韵头和韵尾（黄 & 廖, 2002: 90–92）。

2.3.4 Co-Articulation Effects

We have analyzed the speech sounds in syllables and words. In speaking, we do not utter syllable by syllable. Instead, we move from word to word without stopping. In such a natural speech, when we are pronouncing a phoneme, we are already thinking of the one which follows it. For example, in pronouncing the word *map*, the vowel [æ] is influenced by the preceding nasal consonant [m] and becomes nasalized [æ̃]. Such simultaneous or overlapping articulations in natural speech are called co-articulation effects. The co-articulation effects involve spreading a phonetic property from one sound segment to neighboring segments. The two major types of co–articulation effects in English are assimilation and elision.

2.3.4.1 Assimilation

Assimilation is a phonological process that makes neighboring sound segments more similar by duplicating a phonetic property. Assimilation can occur either within a word or between words, for example:

can [kæ̃n]	washed [wɒʃt]
tan [tæ̃n]	tricks [trɪks]
tenth[tʰɛn̪θ]	impossible [ɪmˈpɒsəbl]
health[hɛl̪θ]	imbalance [ɪmˈbæləns]
sink [siŋk]	ten bucks [tem bʌks]
mink [miŋk]	bad girl [bægˈgɜːl]
map [mæp]	good boy [gʊbˈbɔɪ]
apartment [əˈpɑːpmənt]	love to [lʌf tu]
辛苦[xīŋkǔ]	edge to edge [etʃ tu etʃ]
棉袍 [miam pao]	榆钱儿[yt'yanr]

If a following sound is influencing a preceding sound, we call it regressive assimilation; the converse process, in which a preceding sound is influencing a following sound, is known as progressive assimilation (Spencer, 1996: 47).

In contrast, dissimilation is the change or omission of one of two identical or closely related sounds in a word (https://www.merriam–webster.com/dictionary/dissimilation). For example, the Chinese words 土改, 女子, 了解, 演讲, with the first character of each word changes its tone.

2.3.4.2 Elision

Elision is the omission of sounds, syllables or words (usu. unstressed vowels or medial consonants) in speech. This is done to make the language easier to say, and faster. For example, *camera* [kamra], *'I don't know'* [aɪ duno], *second choice* [ˌsekən ˈtʃɔɪs], *old man* [ˌəʊlˈmæn], *best people* [ˌbesˈpiːpl], *left behind* [ˌlefbɪˈhaɪnd], *fish 'n' chips* are all examples of elision. For Chinese learners, elision is an important area in English listening skills, as learners are often unable to hear elided words correctly, especially if they have little contact with native speakers.

Further Readings:

Clark, John &Colin, Yallop. 1995. *An Introduction to Phonetics and Phonology 2nd Edition.* Oxford: Blackwell. (Reprinted by Foreign Language Teaching and Research Press in 2000)

Gimson, A. C. & Alan Cruttenden. 2001. *Gimson's Pronunciation of English 6th Edition.* London: Arnold. (Reprinted by Foreign Language Teaching and Research Press in 2001)

Roach, Peter. 2000. *English Phonetics and Phonology: A Practical Course 3rd Edition.* Cambridge: Cambridge University Press. (Second edition reprinted by Foreign Language Teaching and Research Press in 2000)

Roach, Peter. 2001. *Phonetics.* Oxford: Oxford University Press. (Reprinted by Shanghai Foreign Language Education Press in 2003)

Yule, G. 2006. *The Study of Language 3rd Edition.* Cambridge:

Cambridge University Press.

黄伯荣 & 廖序东 . 2002.《现代汉语》. 北京：高等教育出版社 .

Questions and Exercises:

1.Define the following terms:

(articulatory) phonetics, phonology, International Phonetic Alphabet, consonant, vowel, cardinal vowels, broad and narrow transcription, minimal pair, phoneme, allophone, complementary distribution, syllable, Maximal Onset Principle, suprasegmentals

2.Give the description of the following consonants in English.

1) [ð]   2) [k]   3) [ʃ]   4) [l]   5) [ŋ]

6) [p]   7) [d]   8) [f]   9) [z]   10) [dʒ]

3.How is phonetics related to phonology and how do they differ from each other?

4.How are consonants classified in the English language?

5.What are co-articulation effects? Illustrate them with your own examples.

6.List the 声母（initial consonants） and 韵母（simple or compound vowel (of a Chinese syllable), sometimes with a terminal [n] or [ng]） in《汉语拼音方案》(*Scheme for the Chinese Phonetic Alphabet*), and illustrate the unique sound patterning rules of Chinese Putonghua with examples.

7.Summarize the different sound patterns of Chinese and English.

Chapter 3

Morphology: The Word Structure of Language

语 言 学 导 论
新文科思政教程

3.1 Introduction

Language has its distinctive feature of duality. It has two levels of structure, and each level has its own principles of organization. Language can be primarily analyzed in terms of combinations of meaningful units (words and morphemes), and secondarily analyzed in terms of meaningless segments (phonemes). We have studied the sounds and sound patterns of English and Chinese in Chapter 2. In Chapter 3, we will learn morphology, which is the study of the internal structure of words and the rules by which words are formed.

Learning Objectives:

1. Remember the following terms: lexeme, word, lexical word, grammatical word, morphology, morpheme, allomorph, free morpheme, bound morpheme, root, affix, stem, base, inflection, compounding, derivation, conversion, backformation, initialism, acronymy, blending, lexical borrowing

2. Understand: the contrast of word formation processes between Chinese and English

3. Illustrate with examples: word formation processes in English

4. Tell stories: special features of Chinese word formation

Lead-in Questions:

1. What is a word? Can you tell the differences of word-formation and

inflection between Chinese and English?

2. Find out what do the following abbreviated terms stand for: *SARS, Covid-19, GPS, AI, app, MOOC, SPOC, GOAT*; and consider what word formation processes are used.

3. Find out the English expressions for the following Chinese terms: *"北斗""一带一路""支付宝""抖音""拼多多""国药""科兴"*. Do foreigners know them?

3.2 The Nature of Words

What is a word? It is a basic unit of language in our everyday speech and writing. We can find theories of word formations, yet hardly do we find a definition of word. The following are several definitions of word:

1. A morpheme or combination of morphemes which native speakers regard as a minimal pronounceable meaningful unit (Wardhaugh, 1986: 222).

2. A word is the smallest unit that one thinks of as being basic to saying anything (Stockwell and Minkova 2001: 56).

3. A linguistic form, as actually uttered, always contains a grammatical form. The grammatical forms of a language can be grouped into three great classes: 1) when a form is spoken alone (that is, not as a constituent of a larger form), it appears in some *sentence-type*, for example, "John!" ⋯ a word is a minimum free form (Bloomfield, 1933:176–177, 186).

4. 词是最小的能够独立运用的语言单位（黄 & 廖 , 2002: 253）。

To put things together, a word is the smallest free unit of language that unite sounds with meaning. Lexicon can refer to all the words and phrases used in a particular language (synonymous with vocabulary). *Oxford Dictionary 2nd Edition* has 273,000 headwords (a word used as a heading of an entry), 171,476 of them being in current use and others of them are obsolete words or derivative words included as subentries. The dictionary contains 157,000 combinations and derivatives in bold type, and 169,000 phrases and combinations in bold italic type, making a total of over 600,000 word-forms (Oxford English Dictionary, Second Edition, Volume 1. Oxford University Press, 1989). There is one count that puts the English vocabulary at about 1 million words — but that count presumably includes words such as Latin species names, prefixed and suffixed words, scientific terminology, jargon, foreign words of extremely limited English use and technical acronyms (https://en.wikipedia.org/wiki/List_of_ dictionaries_by_number_of_words).

A lexeme is the abstract unit underlying the smallest unit in the lexical system of a language, which appears in different grammatical contexts. A lexeme is an entry in a dictionary. A lexeme LEARN includes all of its grammatical forms: *learn, learns, learning, learned, learned.*

Words can be classified into lexical words and grammatical words. Lexical words are words which refer to substance, action and quality and which have lexical meanings or semantic content, such as nouns, verbs, adjectives, and adverbs. Lexical words are also called content words. Grammatical words, also called function words, express grammatical meanings, such as conjunctions, prepositions, articles, and pronouns.

Lexical words belong to open-class words whose membership is in principle infinite or unlimited. With the development of science and technology, inventions and discoveries take place. Thus, new words are added constantly to the current lexicon. In contrast, the membership of grammatical words is fixed or limited. So grammatical words belong to closed-class words.

According to traditional grammar, words can be classified into mainly nine word classes, such as noun, pronoun, verb, adjective, adverb, preposition, conjunction, article and interjection.

"Words may be divided in most languages into variable words and invariable words" (Robins, 1959: 121). Inflection is very common in modern English. English words can be classified into variable words and invariable words. Variable words have inflective changes to show different grammatical meanings of words, such as nouns, pronouns, verbs, adjectives, adverbs. While invariable words don't have inflective endings, such as prepositions, conjunctions, articles and interjections. As an analytic language, Chinese does not have inflection. None of the Chinese words change their endings to express grammatical meanings.

3.3 Word and Its Components in Chinese

3.3.1 Word

汉语词类划分及英汉词类对比

词是最小的能够独立运用的语言单位（黄 & 廖 , 2002: 253）。照汉语语法的老传统，词可粗略分为实词和虚词。以意义为标准，意义实在的叫实词，意义空灵的叫虚词。现在把功能作为主要依据，能够单独充当句法成分，有词汇意义、语法意义的是实词，不能充当句法成分、只有语法意义的就是虚词。实词再细分为名词、动词、形容词、区别词、数词、量词、副词、代词以及特殊实词拟声词、叹词；虚词再细分为介词、连词、助词、语气词。

在词类上，汉语词汇与英语词汇区别如下：1）汉语形容词常作谓语或谓语中心语，如*环境很优美*。2）汉语有区别词，表示事物的属性，有分类的作用，如：男/女、雄/雌、民用/军用、大型/中型、小型/微型等。如*民用*的比较贵。他要买*微型*的。3）汉语量词使用普遍，使语言表达更具体，如一弯新月、一钩晓月、一丝微笑、一只羊、两条狗、一片痴情、万缕霞光。4）汉语没有冠词。5）汉语介词大都由及物动词虚化而来。有的介词与动词同形，只能根据语境和意义判别它是动词还是介词，如他*给我*买书（介词）。他*给我*一本书（动词）（黄 & 廖，2002: 8–39）。

3.3.2 Morpheme

在汉语中，语素是语言中最小的音义结合体（叶 & 徐，1997: 92；黄 & 廖，2002: 251）。就汉语来说，大抵一个汉字就是一个语素，但也有两个字表示一个语素的，如"玻璃、葡萄"，单独汉字无意义。再如，"马虎"是一个语素，语音形式是 [ma3 hu5]，意义是"不认真"；单独汉字"马"和"虎"无意义，不同于"马蹄、马车、马鞍、老虎、猛虎、东北虎"（黄 & 廖，2002: 251）。

汉字始终是一种文字，是符合文字和语言的关系这一规律的。

不能说因为汉字侧重于表义，就认为汉字就是一种可以脱离汉语而存在的，可以"看"得懂而不需要和字音、和语言相联系的符号系统。

汉字与汉语的特点是相适应的。汉语语素以单音节为主要形式，一个语素用一个音节表示，虽然一个音节不是固定地表示某个语素，还有许多同音语素，但语素的单音节形式确是客观存在的事实。汉字也是记录音节的，一个字独立地表示一个音节（但与音节不是对应关系），也正好记录一个语素，与汉语语素的特点相适应。同时，由于汉字与语素基本上对应，而不固定地与某个音节挂钩，所以正好适应了汉语方言分歧的特点，使得汉字具有了超方言的特性。

依据语素的组合能力（构词能力），语素可分为：能够独立成词的语素叫成词语素，如"地、牛、走、跑、又、不、我、你、够、重、远"；不能单独成词的语素叫不成词语素，如"民、语、伟、丰、境、奋、荣、羽、固、阐、瞰"。这两种语素组成新词时表示词的基本意义成为该词的词根。另有一类不成词语素同别的语素组合成词时，位置是固定的，只表示一些附加的意义，又叫词缀，如阿、子、性、者、家（画家、作家）、员（演员、会员）、儿（花儿、鱼儿）。

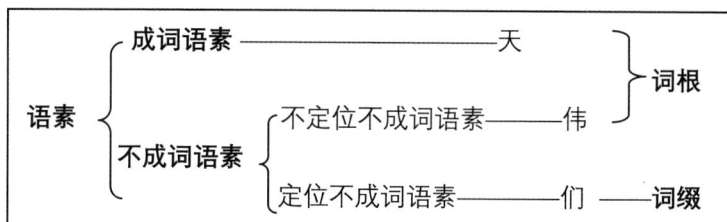

表 3.1 汉语语素与词根、词缀的关系（黄伯荣 & 廖序东，252）

3.4 The Structure of Words

Words are the smallest free unit of language that unite sounds with meaning. Words can be further analyzed into smaller components. In terms of sound, a word can be firstly divided into syllable(s), and secondarily into phonemes. We have analyzed the sound patterns of English and Chinese in Chapter 2. In terms of meaning, a word can be divided into minimal units of meaning in a language – morphemes. For example:

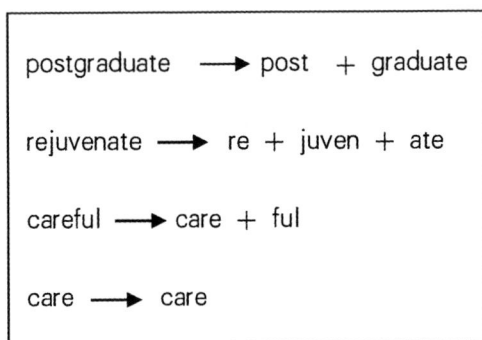

```
postgraduate  ⟶  post + graduate

rejuvenate  ⟶  re + juven + ate

careful  ⟶  care + ful

care  ⟶  care
```

A morpheme is the smallest unit of language in terms of the relationship between expression and content, and cannot be further divided into smaller units without destroying or drastically altering the meaning, whether it is lexical or grammatical. The word *careful* can be analyzed into *care* and *–ful*, which are morphemes. But *care* cannot be divided into *c* and *are*. There are no relations between the parts *c*, *are* and the whole *care*. Therefore, a word may be analyzed into one or more morphemes.

3.4.1 Morpheme, Morph and Allomorph

A morpheme is an abstract concept. Because a morpheme is

represented in both sound and written levels, a morpheme has its concrete forms in different morphological and phonological conditions. The concrete form of a morpheme is called morph. Like phones are the actual phonetic realization of phoneme, we can propose morphs as the actual forms used to realize morphemes (Yule, 2000: 79). The morphs that represent a morpheme in different morphological or phonological conditions are called allomorphs of that morpheme. For example, the English inflectional morpheme *– (e)s* of *books, dogs, boxes, horses* has the same meaning of PLURALITY, yet it has three phonological forms: [*–s, –z, –iz*]. These three forms are variants or allomorphs of the same morpheme *–s*. Another example is the negative prefix *in–* which has its allomorphs *il–, im–, ir–*: *il–* before *l* (e.g. *illegal*); *im–* before *p, b,* or *m* (e.g. *impossible, imbalance, immortal*); *ir–* before *r* (e.g. *irregular*); *in–* before all other consonants and vowels (e.g. *inaccurate, inconvenience, indifferent, inexperienced, invisible*). Even morpheme can be analyzed into morphs, we often use the term "morpheme" for convenience when we actually refer to a morph.

3.4.2 Classification of Morphemes

Morphemes can be classified into different types according to different criteria. In general, there are two main types of classifications.

3.4.2.1 Free Morphemes and Bound Morphemes

A free morpheme is a morpheme that can stand by itself as a single word, e.g. *faith, great, man, water* and *berry*. A word that consists of a single morpheme is called a simple word. A word that consists of two or more free morphemes is called a compound word, e.g. *blackboard, moonwalk, sunflower, self-reliance*. A bound morpheme is a morpheme that cannot stand on its own as a word. They must appear with at least one other morpheme, free or bound, for example, *-ible* in *responsible*; *-ment* in *commitment*; *-ship* in *friendship*; *-es* in *boxes*; *dis-* in *discover*; and *-ceive* in *receive*. A word that consists either of a free morpheme with one or more than one bound morpheme, or of two bound morphemes is called a complex word, e.g. *dogs, careful, atomic, perceive, bookishness*.

3.4.2.2 Roots and Affixes

Poly-morphemic words may be divided into roots and affixes. A root is a form which is not further analyzable, either in terms of derivational or inflectional morphology. It is that part of a word-form that remains when all the inflectional affixes and derivational affixes have been removed, e.g. *friend* in *unfriendliness*. A root may be a free morpheme, e.g. *nation* in *international*, or a bound morpheme, e.g. *-ceive* in *receive, conceive, perceive; -mit* in *remit, permit, commit, submit*.

An affix is the type of morpheme (or formative) that can be used only when added to another morpheme. So, an affix is naturally a bound morpheme. Normally, there are three types of affixes in English: prefix which is placed at the beginning of a word, e.g. *dis-, un-, tele-, sub-*; suffix which is placed at the end of a word, e.g. *-en, -ify, -ful, -less*; and an infix which is placed within a word. Infixes are relatively rare in

English, though we can find examples like *s* in *passersby, mothers–in–law*.

A stem is the part of the word form which remains when all inflectional affixes have been removed (Bauer, 1983: 20), for example, in the word form *friends,* the stem is *friend*; in the word form *writing,* the stem is *write* ; and in the word form *possibilities,* the stem is *possibility*.

A base is the part of the word form that a derivational affix is attached. It may also be defined as "a form to which a rule of word formation is applied." (Bauer, 1983: 20), for example, in the word *unfriendliness*, the base is *unfriendly*; in the word *unfriendly*, the base is *friendly*; and in the word *friendly*, the base is *friend*. Any root or stem can be termed a base.

An affix can be either derivational or inflectional. A derivational affix serves to alter the meaning of a word by building on a base. All prefixes in English are derivational. However, suffixes may be either derivational or inflectional. An inflectional affix adds a minute or delicate grammatical meaning to the stem. But an inflectional affix does not change the part of speech of the stem, nor does it form a new word when it is added to a stem. There are a large number of derivational affixes in English. In contrast, inflectional affixes are limited in English. The following are the major inflectional suffixes in English with their corresponding grammatical functions.

–s	noun plural
–'s	noun possessive
–s	verb present tense third person singular

–ing	verb present participle/gerund
–ed	verb simple past tense
–en	verb past perfect participle
–er	adjective/ adverb comparative
–est	adjective/ adverb superlative

Table 3.2 Inflectional Suffixes in English

3.4.3 Inflection and Word Formation

Inflection is a morphological process in which a word is modified to express different grammatical categories such as tense, case, voice, aspect, person, number, gender, mood, and definiteness. An inflection expresses grammatical categories with affixation or other modifications (Brinton, 2000:104). Inflection does not change the part of speech of the word, nor does it create a new word. But due to the fact that inflection plays an important role in an English sentence, i.e., the tense, agreement, and other grammatical categories are realized through inflection, inflection is an important part of English grammar.

Word formation is the process of forming new words. There are three main kinds of word formation in English: derivation, conversion and compounding. Other word–formation processes in English include abbreviation, back–formation, lexical borrowing and coinage (https:// dictionary.cambridge.org/grammar/british–grammar/word–formation_2).

3.5 Word Formation Processes in English

With the development of science and technology, inventions and discoveries have changed our lives significantly. For example, the word *digital* means "recording or storing information as a series of the numbers 1 and 0", e.g. *a digital camera*. It has been enriched with a new meaning of "using or relating to computers and the internet", as in expressions like *the digital age, digital divide, digital economy*. The former meaning of *digital* is connected with the 1950's world of computers, and the new meaning arises in the context of the Internet of Things. The word *digital* started from Latin *digitalis* (from *digitus* "finger or toe") in the mid−17th century, with original meanings of "pertaining to numbers below ten", or "pertaining to fingers" (https://www.etymonline.com/word/digital).

A new word or expression, which is referred to as a neologism, can be a coinage that is a word or phrase recently invented, or a word used with a new meaning. New words are formed according to morphological rules that determine how morphemes combine to form new words in a language. In English, there are three main kinds of word formation: compounding, derivation, and conversion; and minor word formation processes, such as abbreviation, back−formation, lexical borrowing and coinage. According to G. Leech (1981), percentage of new words coined by the different word−formation processes after WWII were: compounding (about 27%), e.g. *blueprint*; derivation (about 17.5%), e.g. *modernize*; conversion (about 10.5%), e.g. *bottle (v.)*. The three main processes accounted for 55% of the new vocabulary; and abbreviations (about 19%), e.g. *UNESCO,*

U.N., brunch, phone; and borrowing (about 18.5%), e.g. *discotheque*. While a recent research which took *Oxford English Dictionary (OED) Online (2012–2016)* as a corpus found that the most productive process of creating English new words was affixation, followed by folk etymology, compounding, abbreviation, acronymy, borrowing, blending, clipping, and back−formation (https://www.researchgate.net/publication/331870463_ WORD_FORMATION_PROCESSES_IN_ENGLISH_NEW_WORDS_OF_OXFORD_ ENGLISH_DICTIONARY_OED_ONLINE).

3.5.1 Derivation

Derivation, also called "affixation", is the process of creating a new word by adding an affix to a base (or root). Affixation can be subdivided into prefixation, the addition of a prefix to a base to make a new word, e.g., *discover, empower*; and suffixation, the formation of a new word by adding a suffix to a base, e.g. *digitize, colorful*. The word *international* is the result of both prefixation and suffixation. Derivations can make the word class of the original word either changed or unchanged. The following table shows examples of affixation in English.

Affix	Base	Derived word	Word class
a-	symmetric	asymmetric	Adj.
anti-	inflammatory	anti-inflammatory	Adj.
auto-	mobile	automobile	N.
bi-	cycle	bicycle	N.

co-	operation	cooperation	N.
contra-	diction	contradiction	N.
counter-	measure	countermeasure	N.
dis-	appear	disappear	V.
hyper-	tension	hypertension	N.
il-	logical	illogical	Adj.
im-	mortal	immortal	Adj.
in-	active	inactive	Adj.
ir-	regular	irregular	Adj.
infra-	red	infrared	N.
inter-	national	international	Adj.
macro-	economics	macroeconomics	N.
mal-	nutrition	malnutrition	N.
meta-	verse	metaverse	N.
micro-	meter	micrometer	N.
mis-	spelling	misspelling	N.
mono-	-logue	monologue	
multi-	lateral	multilateral	Adj.
non-	stop	nonstop	V. →Adj.
poly-	ester	polyester	N.
post-	COVID-19	post-COVID-19	N.
pre-	historic	prehistoric	Adj.
pro-	noun	pronoun	N.
pseudo-	name	pseudonym	N.

re-	-ceive	receive	
semi-	conductor	semiconductor	N.
sub-	marine	submarine	Adj.
super-	market	supermarket	N.
trans-	Atlantic	transatlantic	Adj.
ultra-	violet	ultraviolet	N.
un-	able	unable	Adj.
xeno-	phobia	xenophobia	N.
-able/-ible	drink reduce	drinkable reducible	V. →Adj.
-al	recreation	recreational	N.→Adj.
-ant	ignore	ignorant	V. →Adj.
-ess	actor	actress	N.
-ful	beauty	beautiful	N. →Adj.
-fy	glory	glorify	N. →V.
-hood	neighbor	neighborhood	N.
-ic	poet	poetic	N. →Adj.
-ise/-ize	digit	digitize	N. →V.
-ish	grey self	greyish selfish	Adj. N. →Adj.
-ism	Marx cake	Marxism cakeism(OED 2018)	N.
-ist	biology	biologist	N.
-less	color	colorless	N. →Adj.
-like	child	childlike	N. →Adj.

-ment	move	movement	V. →N.
-ness	slow	slowness	Adj. →N.
-tion/ -sion	civilize	civilization	V. →N.

Table 3.3 Examples of Affixation in English

From the above examples in Table 3.3, we can see some properties of derivation in English. First, most words derived through prefixation have the same part of speech as the base, while most words derived through suffixation have a different part of speech from the base. Second, derivational affixes are influenced by phonological factors, for example, the negative prefix *in–* has allomorphs of *il–, im–, in–,　ir–* in different phonetic environments as illustrated in Table 3.3. Third, the suffixed words are generally stressed on the syllable before the suffix, for example, *classic [ˈklæsɪk], metallic [mə ˈtælɪk], economic [ˌiːkə ˈnɒmɪk], enthusiastic [ɪnˌθjuːzi ˈæstɪk]* are all stressed on the syllable before the suffix *–ic*.

3.5.2 Compounding

Compounding or composition is a word formation process consisting of joining two or more words to form a new unit, a compound word or a compound, e.g. *blueprint, homesick, bittersweet, clear–cut.*

In English, words can be combined in various ways to form compounds. In terms of word class, English compounds are mainly noun compounds, verb compounds, and adjective compounds as shown in Table 3.4.

	-Noun	-Verb	-Adjective
Noun-	grassroot steamboat sunset power plant pathway dogdays	breastfeed birth control daybreak headache heartbeat lip-read	tax-free homesick fire-proof watertight crystal-clear
Verb-	breakfast cutthroat pickpocket know-nothing	sleepwalk click clack snapshot	blow-dry spin-dry
Adjective-	blackbird blueprint blue blood white-collar green policy software T-shirt black-hole	dry-clean whitewash clear-cut remote-control	bittersweet Anglo-French deaf-mute dark blue

Table 3.4 Examples of Compounding in English

Generally, we can see motivation from English compounds in terms of meaning and word class. The meaning and word class are usually determined by the second or final word of a compound as the head of the compound. It is an endocentric compound, a type of compound in which one member functions as the head and the other as its modifier, attributing a property to the head. The endocentric compound and its head are of the relationship of "a kind of", e.g. *steamboat, sunset, lip-read, software, black hole, remote control.*

In contrast, there is compound that lacks a head word: That is, the construction as a whole is not grammatically and/or semantically equivalent to either of its parts. It is called an exocentric compound, or a headless compound, e.g. *cutthroat, pickpocket, blue blood.*

Compounds differ from phrases in terms of stress patterns. A compound is usually stressed on the first part. While a phrase is usually stressed on the last part. For example, *a 'blackbird* is a special kind of bird, while *a black 'bird* is any bird that is black.

Compounds are written in different ways. Some can be written as a solid word, such as *blackboard, breakfast, headache, homesick, bittersweet*; some can be hyphenated, such as, *T-shirt, clear-cut, Anglo-French, lip-read*; some can be written with ordinary space within the two parts, such as *green policy, blue blood, dark blue.*

3.5.3 Conversion

Conversion is a word-formation process by which a word is altered from one part of speech into another without the addition (or deletion) of any morpheme. This process is also called functional shift or derivation by zero suffix. English had lost most of its inflectional endings by the end of Middle English period (1066- the late 15th century), which facilitated the use of words interchangeably as verbs or nouns, verbs or adjectives, and vice versa. The free interchange of a word from one word class to another is a significant feature of Modern English. The following are common conversions in English.

1)noun → verb

adult: e.g. Adulting is hard (adulting is a word of the year 2016 in OED online https://languages.oup.com/word−of−the−year/2016−shortlist/).

orbit: e.g. Mercury orbits the Sun.

distance: e.g. social distancing (a word of the year 2020 in OED online)

bomb: Zoombombing (a word of the year 2020 in OED online)

message: e.g. to message

e−mail: e.g. to e−mail

host: e.g. to host a meeting

cash: e.g. to cash a cheque

2)adjective → verb

mute: e.g. to mute and unmute yourself on Zoom

slim: e.g. Some people try to slim down via diet.

dim: e.g. the lights dimmed

mature: e.g. Age matures a good wine.

empty: e.g. to empty

3)adjective → noun

deaf: e.g. the deaf and the blind

oppressed: e.g. the oppressed

native: e.g. a returned native

high/ low: e.g. reach a new high/ low

right/ wrong: e.g. to know the difference between right and wrong

4)verb → noun

doubt: e.g. beyond doubt

produce: e.g. farm produce

pass: e.g. a pass

treat: e.g. treat or trick

divide: e.g. digital divide

retreat: e.g. a retreat

3.5.4 Abbreviation

Abbreviation or shortening is a word formation process by shortening a word or a phrase, by any method. Abbreviations are created to avoid spelling out whole words. They help make a cumbersome text concise. We can find abbreviations in the following ways in English.

Clipping is the deletion of one or more syllables from a word (usu. a noun), which is also available in its full form, for example, shortened forms of English names like *Bob (Robert), Liz (Elizabeth), Cathy (Catherine)*. We can divide clippings in three types: back−clippings like *expo (exposition), exam (examination), kilo (kilogram), Hi−Fi (high fidelity), mike/mic (microphone)*; fore−clippings like *bus (omnibus), burger (hamburger), quake (earthquake), phone (telephone)*; and fore−and−aft clippings like *flu (influenza), tec (detective)*.

Initialism is a type of shortening, using the first letters of words to form a proper name, a technical term, or a phrase. An initialism is pronounced letter by letter, for example, *ATM (Automated Teller Machine)*, *AI (artificial intelligence)*, *GDP (Gross Domestic Product)*, *PR (public relations)*, *CAI (Computer-Assisted Instruction)*, *GPS (Global Positioning System)*, *BRI (Belt and Road Initiative)*.

Acronymy is the process of forming new words by joining the initial letters of the name of an organization or a scientific term. Words formed in this way are called acronyms, which differ from initialisms in that they are pronounced as words rather than as sequences of letters, for example, *APEC (Asia-Pacific Economic Cooperation)*, *UNESCO (United Nations Educational, Scientific and Cultural Organization)*, *WASP (White Anglo-Saxon Protestant)*, *AIDS (Acquired Immunodeficiency Syndrome)*.

Blending is a process of word formation in which a new word is formed by combining the meanings and sounds of two words, one of which is not in its full form or both of which are not in their full forms, for example, *smog (smoke +fog)*, *comsat (communications satellite)*, *COVID-19 (Corona Virus Disease of 2019)*, *Brexit (British +Exit)*, *medicare (medical +care)*, *Ms. (Miss +Mrs.)*.

3.5.5 Backformation

Backformation is a process of word formation by the deletion of an imagined affix from a longer form already in the language, for example, *edit (editor)*, *babysit (babysitter)*, *air-condition (air-conditioner)*, *burgle (burglar)*, *peddle (peddler)*, *hawk (hawker)*, *emote (emotion)*, *brainwash (brainwashing), sightsee (sightseeing).*

3.5.6 Invention/ Coinage

Besides, there is also invention/ coinage of new words from brand names or other technological and economic activities, for example, *Kodak, Coke, nylon, Band—aid, Xerox, Lycra, Simmons, granola, ipad, TikTok, Alipay, eco—civilization.*

3.5.7 Borrowing

Borrowing or lexical borrowing is the process by which a word from one language is adapted for use in another. In English, there are many words borrowed from other languages. Borrowed words can be classified into four types: the borrowing of loanwords is a process in which both form and meaning are borrowed with only a slight adaptation, e.g., *au pair, encore, coup d'etat, kungfu, sputnik*; loanblending is a process in which part of the form is native and part is borrowed, but the meaning is fully borrowed, for example, *coconut* ← *coco (Spanish) + nut (English), Chinatown* ← *China (Chinese) + town (English)*; loanshift is a process in which the meaning is borrowed, but the form is native, e.g. *bridge (*meaning as a card game borrowed from Italian *ponte)*; and loan translation is a special type of borrowing in which each word is translated in the equivalent word in another language, e.g. *black humor* (from French word *humor noir*), *free verse* (from Latin *verse libre).*

3.6 Word Formation Processes in Chinese

汉语中,词由一个或几个语素构成。构词语素分两种,一种叫词根,指意义实在、在合成词内位置不固定的不成词语素和成词语素;一种叫词缀,指意义不实在、在合成词内位置固定在前或在后的不成词语素(见表3.1)。汉语构词法从不同角度有不同的分类:1)在语音方面,从音节的多少可以分为单音节词和多音节词;从音节间的结构关系可以分为重叠式和非重叠式。2)从词素多少和词素性质方面,可以分为一个词素构成的单纯词和两个或两个以上词素构成的合成词。

3.6.1 Compounding and Affixation

3.6.1.1 合成法:将两个或两个以上的语素组合成新词的方法。

联合式:由意义相同、相近或相反的语素并列组合而成。例如*波浪、语言、遥远、干旱;是非、多少、反正、始终、伸缩*。

偏正式:前一个语素对后一个语素加以修饰限制。例如*深夜、茶杯、漆黑、重视、旁观、单干、徒手、梅花鹿、中山装、生产力*。

主谓式:前一语素为陈述对象,后一语素对之加以陈述。例如*脸红、心跳、地震、认为、肉麻、眼看、胆小*。

动宾式:前一语素表示行为或动作,后一语素表示其对象。例如*讲理、操心、说谎、示威、捐款、公关、照样、到底*。

补充式:后一语素对前一语素加以补充说明。例如*改正、说明、打开、治安、提前、赶快、趁早、分明、月季花、茅台酒、梅花、鲤鱼、船只、纸张、米粒、花束*。

3.6.1.2 附加法 / 加缀法:指通过在词根前加前缀或在其后面加后缀构造新词的方法。汉语前后缀数量不如英语那样多,也没那么固定，多数由词根转化而来。汉语往往一缀一意。汉语加缀法构成的词数量有限，如前缀：老、小、阿、第、非、初（如*老虎、老鹰、阿姨、初十*）。后缀：儿、子、头、者、员、家、然、乎、巴、于、性、度、率、化（如*画家、花儿、演员、锄头、儿子、姑娘家、属于、合乎、忽然*）。

3.6.2 Reduplication

重叠法：通过将语素重叠构造新词的方法。

汉语中的重叠词形式多、数量大、极为常用。从重叠词的词性上，可分为名词重叠、动词重叠、形容词重叠和量词重叠。例如名词重叠表示"每个、所有"的意义（*家家、户户、人人*）；动词重叠表示"语气轻松、动作反复、时间短"的意义（*说说、瞧瞧、歇歇、娓娓、谆谆、哗哗、考虑考虑、讨论讨论、吵吵嚷嚷*）；形容词重叠表示"程度的加深或表达某种感情色彩"（*喋喋、冉冉、大大的、红红的、高高的、白茫茫、冷冰冰、静悄悄、干干净净、漂漂亮亮、密密麻麻、战战兢兢、蜡黄蜡黄*）；量词重叠表示"每一""逐个"或某种感情色彩（*个个、件件、场场、条条*）。

由以上分析可以看出：1）汉语构词法和英语构词法都包含单纯词构词法、合成构词法和词缀构词法。2）与英语构词法不同，重叠构词法是汉语比较突出的一种构词法（许余龙，2010: 85）。3）汉语属于分析语，词性灵活，兼类词以及词性活用比比皆是，句子表达重在表意。比如吃食堂、吃饭、晒太阳、晒被子、看医生、看病；再如下面汉英词汇"清楚"：

清楚十分重要。 她的解释很清楚。 大家都喜欢清楚。 她做了清楚的解释。 她清楚地做了解释。 她解释得很清楚。	She made a clear explanation. The explanation is quite clear. The explanation must be made clear.

3.6.3 The Fusion of Chinese and English Morphemes in the Language Contact

汉语倾向于具体，英语倾向于抽象（连淑能，1993: 128）。汉语的一些抽象词缀（如*性、度、率、化、主义*）多来自外语，尤其是英语。在使用中，这些词缀的用法也在不断发展，与汉语融合。"化"在《现代汉语词典》（第6版）中的释义：（8）后缀，加在名词或形容词之后构成动词，表示转变成某种性质或状态。"化"来源于英语后缀"-fy, –ize, –en"，如*简化、工业化、机械化、数字化、强化*（simplify, industrialize, mechanize, digitize, strengthen）；但，"化"的组合功能有所发展和扩大，如*经常化、绝对化、高学历化、绿化、美化、老龄化、年轻化*。"吧"（[ba1]）在《现代汉语词典》（第6版）中以词条出现【区别于词条吧 [ba1]（动词）和吧 [ba5]（语气助词）】，指（1）酒吧：吧台。（2）供人从事某些休闲活动的场所，有的兼售酒水、食品：网吧、氧吧。释义1解释了"吧"源于英语 bar，释义2是"吧"在汉语中用法的发展。再如"门"：来源于*水门事件*（Watergate Scandal, 1972）。与《现代汉语词典》（第5版）相比，《现代汉语

词典》（第 6 版）(2012) 在"门"释义中增加了新义项：（10）借指
公众关注的消极事件，如贿赂门、考试门。

Further Readings:

Adams, V. 1973. *An Introduction to Modern English Word-Formation*. London: Longman.

Bauer, Laurie. 1983. *English Word-Formation*. London: Cambridge University Press.

Carstairs-McCarthy, A. 2002. *An Introduction to English Morphology: Words and Their Structure*. Edinburgh: Edinburgh University Press.

Matthews, P.H. 2000. *Morphology (2nd Edition)*. 北京：外语教学与研究出版社 .

Radford, A. et al. 2000. *Linguistics: An Introduction*. 北京：外语教学与研究出版社 .

汪榕培 , 2013.《英语词汇学》（十一五国家级规划教材）. 上海：上海外语教育出版社 .

杨信彰 , 2009.《英语词汇学教程》（十一五国家级规划教材）. 北京 : 高等教育出版社 .

Questions and Exercises:

1.Define the following terms:

lexeme, word, lexical word, grammatical word, morphology, morpheme, allomorph, free morpheme, bound morpheme, root, affix, stem, base, inflection, word formation, compounding, derivation, conversion, backformation, initialism, acronymy, blending, lexical borrowing

2. How is morpheme classified?

3. Use your own examples to illustrate the word formation processes in English.

4. Use examples to tell the cultural story of words derived through backformation in English, e.g., baby-sitter.

5. 叠音拟声词使《诗经》描写具体而生动。阅读以下诗句，思考如何译为英语？

水声："河水洋洋，北流活活。"（《卫风·硕人》）

鸟声："关关雎鸠，在河之洲。"（《周南·关雎》）

鹿鸣声："呦呦鹿鸣，食野之苹。"（《小雅·鹿鸣》）

伐木声："坎坎伐檀兮，置之河之干兮。"（《国风·魏风·伐檀》）

Chapter 4

Syntax: The Sentence Structure of Language

语 言 学 导 论
新文科思政教程

4.1 Introduction

According to Bloomfield, a word is a minimum free form and a sentence is a maximum free form. "It is evident that the sentences in any utterance are marked off by the mere fact that each sentence is an independent linguistic form, not included by virtue of any grammatical construction in any larger linguistic form" (Bloomfield, 1933: 178). Sentences play an important role in the hierarchical structure of language. A sentence can be uttered alone to convey a thorough idea as an utterance. A sentence can be logically connected with other sentences to form a larger unit as a text to convey more thoughtful ideas. Since we have learned word structure in Chapter 3, we will learn sentence structure and touch a bit of textual grammar in this chapter.

The word "syntax" comes from the ancient Greek sýntaxis, which consists of syn–, "together", and –táxis, "ordering". Syntax literally means "a putting together or in order, arrangement, a grammatical construction". In linguistics, syntax is the study of the rules governing the ways different constituents are combined to form sentences in a language, or the study of the interrelationships between elements in sentence structures.

In English, a sentence is identified with a basic structure of "subject + predicate". It is in accordance with traditional grammar. Saussure and Bloomfield start structural linguistics which puts elements of a sentence in structural relations. Structural grammar demonstrates the dichotomy within a sentence: horizontal and vertical relations, linear and hierarchical relations, construction and constituents. Even structural approach has its advantages, it fails to explain deep syntactic relations, which is later solved by Transformational–Generative Grammar (TG grammar). As the founder of TG Grammar, Chomsky gives us a psychological point of view concerning a speaker's ideal knowledge of language and his actual language performance. TG grammar explains the generative mechanism of human Language Acquisition Device (LAD) through phrase structure rules and transformations (transformational rules). Its emphasis on the generative power of human innate language capacity (the Universal Grammar) calls linguists' attention to psycholinguistics which has benefited us with a lot of cutting–edge inventions such as machine translation, language corpus, AI, and robot. In contrast with the formal linguistics, functional linguistics sees that communicative function of language determines the choice of language forms. Functional grammar takes "theme" and "rheme" analysis of a sentence, and thematic progression is effective in text analysis. Systemic–Functional grammar puts emphasis on the system of language and puts forward the three metafunctions of language.

All these different theories are based on the traditional grammar of English sentences.

Learning Objectives:

1. Remember the following terms: syntax, category, sentence, syntagmatic relations, paradigmatic relations, endocentric construction, exocentric construction, coordination, subordination, construction, constituent, IC analysis, deep structure, surface structure, phrase structure rules, transformational rules, X-bar, the six cohesive devices

2. Understand: key notions in different approaches of sentence grammar

3. Illustrate with examples: IC analysis of sentences, esp., those with structural ambiguity; transformational rules; thematic progression; system of meaning potentials

Lead-in Questions:

1. Find examples that violates the traditional English grammars like *You must not split an infinitive.*

2. What are the basic sentence patterns in English? Explain with examples.

3. Try to paraphrase the following two sentences by analyzing the syntactic relationship within each sentence.

   John is easy to please.

   John is eager to please.

4.2 The Traditional Approach to Grammar

Traditional grammar refers to the type of grammar study done prior to the beginnings of modern linguistics. Traditional grammar of English focused on the study of the structure and formation of words and sentences, usually without much reference to sound and meaning. It can be traced back over 2,000 years to Greek and Latin grammar, and later French. The grammars was prescriptive that one variety of a language was laid down as the norm for all speakers of the language. Some familiar examples of prescriptive rules for English sentences are as follows:

1)You must not split an infinitive.

2)You must not end a sentence with a preposition.

3)You should avoid passive voice.

4)You should not start a sentence with a conjunction.

5)When describing an emotion, use of an English word descended from Latin is preferred over an Anglo–Saxon word.

6)Circumlocution and undue emphasis on subtlety may not be as effective a way of getting your message across when more direct and concise framing is preferable. (https://eclecticlight.co/2015/02/01/ rules–for–a–prescriptive–grammar/)

Yule has pointed out that it was inappropriate to apply the first rule of Latin grammar to English. Because Latin infinitives are single words and just do not split, while the infinitive in English has the form *to* + the *verb*, as in *to go* (Yule, 2000: 91).

Even prescriptive rules of grammar are rigid and bothersome, traditional grammar provides many basic concepts for modern linguistics, such as the notion of sentence, grammatical category, agreement and government.

4.2.1 Definition of Sentence

Traditionally, a sentence is "a series of words in connected speech or writing, forming the grammatically complete expression of a single thought" (Matthews, 1981). Actually, this traditional definition of sentence is different from the definition of utterance: a sentence is a theoretical unit defined by a grammar; while an utterance is a physical unit, a matter of production, or performance. A word may be an utterance, like "John!". That is why Bloomfield defined "a word is the minimum free form" (Bloomfield, 1933: 186). What Bloomfield talked about there is in terms of utterance instead of sentence. At the same time, Bloomfield defined a sentence as the maximum free form, "each sentence is an independent linguistic form, not included by virtue of any grammatical construction in any larger linguistic form" (Bloomfield, 1933: 178). A sentence is the largest structural unit to which syntactic rules apply. This definition falls in accord with traditional grammar.

A sentence refers to a set of words that is complete in itself, typically containing a subject and predicate, conveying a statement, question, exclamation, or command, and consisting of a main clause and sometimes one or more subordinate clauses (https://languages.oup.com/google-dictionary-en/). Traditionally, sentences can be classified into three types: simple, compound and complex. A simple sentence contains only one subject–predicate unit. Classification of English sentences in traditional grammar is as follows:

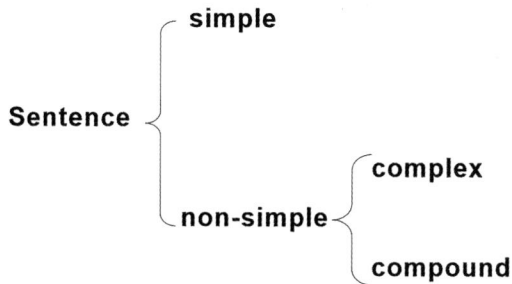

```
                    ┌─ simple
                    │
   Sentence ────────┤
                    │              ┌─ complex
                    └─ non-simple ─┤
                                   └─ compound
```

The basic components of English sentences include subject (S), predicate verb (V), object (O), complement (C) and adverbial (A). There are 6 major declarative sentence patterns in English as follows:

1) John arrived. (SV)

2) Jean looks fine. (SVC)

3) John loves Jean. (SVO)

4) John gives Jean a bunch of flowers. (SVOO)

5) Jean called John honey. (SVOC)

6) There is a cafeteria in the street corner. (There be+ S +A.)

Word order is among the three basic ways (word order, genetic and areal classifications) to classify languages in the world: SVO, VSO, SOV, OVS, OSV, and VOS. English belongs to SVO type, though this does not mean that SVO is the only possible word order in English. Which word order does Chinese belong to?

4.2.2 Grammatical Category

The word **category** can refer to a class or group of things, people, etc, possessing some quality or qualities in common; it can be a division in a system of classification. Categorization or classification is a fundamental human cognition process in knowing the world. It allows human to organize things, objects, and ideas that exist around them and simplify their understanding of the world. In the philosophy of Aristotle, category means any one of ten most fundamental modes of being, such as quantity, quality, and substance. A **grammatical category** refers to classes and functions in its narrow sense, e.g. noun, verb, subject, predicate, etc. More specifically, it refers to the defining properties of a word that can cause that word and/or a related word to change in form for grammatical reasons (ensuring agreement between words): the categories of nouns in English, for example, include number, gender, case and countability; and of verbs, for example, include tense, aspect, and voice. Traditional grammar provides modern linguistics with grammatical categories like parts of speech, subject, predicate, number, gender, case, tense, aspect, and voice.

Number is a grammatical category of nouns, pronouns, adjectives and verb agreement that expresses count distinctions (such as "one" or "more than one"). The count distinctions typically, but not always, correspond to the actual count of the referents of the marked noun or pronoun. In English, the two number categories are singular and plural. These two categories relate to nouns, pronouns, determiners, and verbs.

Type	Number Category	
	Singular Example	Plural Example
Noun	cat, mouse	cats, mice
Pronoun	I, me, you, he, him, she, her, it	we, us, you, they, them
Determiner	this, that, a, an, my, your, his, her, its	these, those, our, your, their
Verb	am, is, was, has, play, plays	are, were, have, play

Case shows a noun's or a pronoun's relationship with the other words in a sentence. The category of case is prominent in Latin grammar. It has six distinctions of nominative, vocative, accusative, genitive, dative and ablative. We can find the first five of them in English. If a noun or pronoun is used as the subject of a verb, it is said to be in the nominative case. If a noun or pronoun is used as the object of a verb, it is said to be in the accusative case. If a noun is used as an indirect object of the verb in a sentence, it is said to be in the dative case. For example: *Mr. Bright taught us English. The flower gives us fragrance.* If a noun denotes the possession or ownership, it is said to be in the possessive or genitive case. For example: *This is Mr. White's car.* If a noun is used to name or call a person or thing addressed, it is said to be in the Vocative case. For example: *Boys, don't go there. Tom, please close the door.*

Gender is a grammatical category in inflected languages governing the agreement between nouns and pronouns and adjectives; in some languages it is quite arbitrary but in Indo–European languages it is usually based on sex or animateness. In English, a noun can have a masculine gender, a feminine gender, or a neuter gender. Gender contrast can only be observed in pronouns and a small number of nouns, and they are mainly of the natural gender type.

Grammatical Gender in English		
Masculine	Feminine	Neuter
bull	cow	calf
ram	ewe	lamb
he	she	it

Agreement (or Concord) may be defined as the requirement that the forms of two or more words in a syntactic relationship should agree with each other in terms of some categories. For example, in English the demonstrative and the noun which follows it should concord in number: *this man, these men, a book, some books*. And subjects and verbs should agree with each other in number in the present tense: *He speaks English. They speak English.* A pronoun should agree with its antecedent in person, number, and gender.

Government is another type of control over the form of some words by other words in certain syntactic constructions. It differs from concord in that this is a relationship in which a word of a certain class determines the form of others in terms of certain category. Verbs and prepositions govern their objects, and more generally, heads govern their dependents. In the general definition of government, a head always governs its immediately adjacent complement: for example, *see the cat: see* governs *the cat.*

on the waterfront: on governs *the waterfront.*

the ruler of the country: ruler governs *of the country.*

proud of one's achievements: proud governs *of one's achievements.*

Besides, we can learn parts of speech of English words in a grammar book. Traditional grammar with its terminologies, categories and its analysis of an English sentence has paved the way for modern linguistics. Modern linguistics differs from traditional grammar in some essential aspects as listed in Chapter 1.

4.2.3 Chinese Grammar

4.2.3.1 汉语句子的结构类——句型

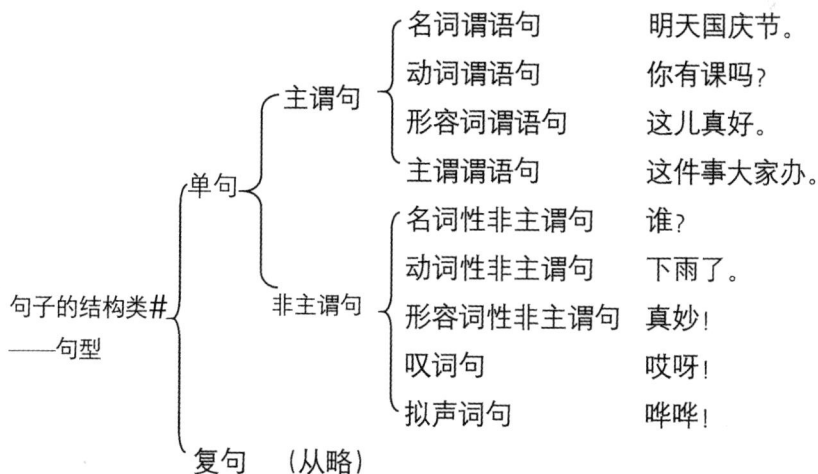

		名词谓语句	明天国庆节。
	主谓句	动词谓语句	你有课吗?
		形容词谓语句	这儿真好。
单句		主谓谓语句	这件事大家办。
		名词性非主谓句	谁?
		动词性非主谓句	下雨了。
	非主谓句	形容词性非主谓句	真妙!
		叹词句	哎呀!
		拟声词句	哗哗!

句子的结构类#——句型

复句　（从略）

（黄 & 廖, 2002: 110）

4.2.3.2 汉语句法与英语不同之处：

1）连谓句：由连谓短语充当谓语或独立成句的句子。如：

表先后发生的动作：*金生取了笔记本走了。*

前后表方式和目的关系：*领导表扬先进树榜样。*

前一动作表方式：*他低着头沉思往事。*

从正反两方面说明一件事：*他俩站着不动。*

后一性状表前一动作的结果：*大家听了很高兴。*

前后两件事表因果关系：*他看书看累了。*

前后有条件和行为的关系：*小二黑有资格谈恋爱。*

表先后发生的动作：*他上车买票。*

2）兼语句：由兼语短语充当谓语或独立成句的句子。根据兼语前一动词的语义，兼语句大致分以下三种：

前一动词有使令意义，能引起一定的结果，常见的动词有"请、使、叫、让、派、催、逼、求、托、命令、吩咐、动员、促使、发动、组织、鼓励、号召"等。如：*微笑使你年轻，使你精神愉快。*

前一动词是表示赞许、责怪或心理活动的及物动词，它是由兼语后面的动作或性状引起的，前后谓语有因果关系。常见的动词有"称赞、表扬、夸、笑、骂、爱、恨、嫌、喜欢、感谢、埋怨"等。如：*我感谢你告诉我一个好消息。*

前一动词有"有、轮"等表示领有或存在等。如：

他有个哥哥在北京工作。

有人找你。

轮到你值班了。

兼语句和连谓句可以出现在一句里。如：

连长去请指导员来接电话。

鲁迅先生派人叫我明天早晨打电话托内山先生请医生看病。

4.3.2.3 汉语句法成分与英语不同之处：

1）主语可分为名词性主语和谓词性主语。这里，谓词性词语包括动词、形容词、谓词性的代词、动词性短语、形容词性短语（含主谓短语）。这是以动作、性状或事情作陈述的对象,这种句子可以叫谓词主语句。如：

动词：*笑是具有多重意义的语言。*

形容词：*骄傲是无知的产物。*

代词：*这样行不行?*

动词联合短语：*信不信由你。*

形容词联合短语：*公正廉洁是公职人员行为的准则。*

动宾短语：*拆台比搭台容易得多。*

主谓短语：*他不参加也好。*

兼语短语：*请他做报告已经不是个新鲜事儿了。*

状中短语：*认真地学习外语是对的。*

中补短语：*学习得认真是应该的。*

连谓短语：*去北京查资料很重要。*

主谓短语：*两国总统互访意义重大。*

谓词性主语句（含主谓主语句）的谓语总是由非动作性谓词（判断动词、形容词等）充当。这不同于名词性主语句中，谓语在词性上不受限制，只要语义能搭配，可以用各种谓词语充当。

2）谓语通常由谓词性词语充当，在一定条件下也可由名词性词语充当。形容词性词语也经常作谓语。形容词作谓语，也常常用复杂形式，如：

今天晚上特别冷。

这样行不行？

这样好。

拆台比搭台容易得多。

形容词单独作谓语，也受一定的条件限制。用在复句的分句里，主要是对比句或先行句、后续句。如：

说有易，说无难。

道远，你多走一会不就得了！

多穿点衣服再出去，外头冷。

不然，句末也要有语气词，如：

我累了。

天晚了。

主谓短语作谓语大致有五种：（1）大主语是受事，小主语是施事，"受事//施事——动作。如：这件事大家都赞成。（2）大主语是施事，小主语是受事，"施事//受事——动作。如：你这个人，//锤都没摸过。（3）大主语和小主语有广义的领属关系。如：他//一向态度和蔼。（4）谓语里有复指大主语的复指成分。如：咱们俩//谁也别忘了谁。（5）大主语前暗含一个介词"对、对于、关于"等等。大主语如果加上介词，就变成句首状语了。如：这三个问题，//我们讨论了两个。

名词性短语作谓语比较少见，有以下四种条件限制：（1）只能是肯定句，不能是否定句；（2）只能是短句，不能是长句；（3）只能是口语句式，不能是书面语句式；（4）限于说明时间、天气、籍贯、年龄、容貌等的口语短句。如：

明天清明节。

鲁迅，浙江绍兴人。

两人一房间。

这本书新买的。

米饭一碗，饮料两瓶。

4.3 The Structural Approach

The structural approach in linguistic study was started by Ferdinand Saussure, the father of modern linguistics, in the beginning of the 20th century. Structural linguistics treats all language units interrelated with each other in a structure or system, not as isolated bits. Every item acquires identity and validity only in relation to the other items in the system. Linguistics of the 20th century is structural in this sense, as opposed to much work in the earlier times.

4.3.1 Syntactic Relations

Saussure sees language signs in SYNTAGMATIC and ASSOCIATIVE relations, and the meaning of language is determined by its relation to other signs, its position in the system. Syntagmatic relations, also called horizontal relations or chain relations, are a relation between one item and others in a sequence, or between elements which are all present, such as the relation between *weather* and the others in the sentence: *If the weather is nice, we'll go out*. There are syntactic and semantic conditions the words in a syntagmatic relation must meet. The associative relations (or in Hjemslev's term paradigmatic relations), also called vertical relations or choice relations, refer to classes or sets of words substitutable for each other grammatically in sentences with the same structure. Words in an associative relation are comparable only in terms of syntax. Semantic factors are not taken into consideration here. A paradigmatic relation also refers to groups of more than one word which may be jointly substitutable grammatically for a single word of a particular set.

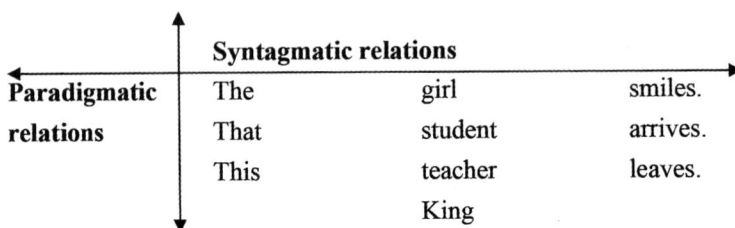

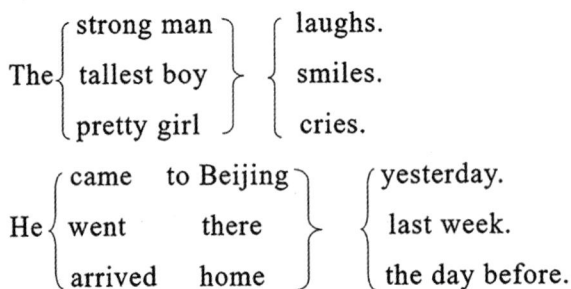

	Syntagmatic relations		
Paradigmatic	The	girl	smiles.
relations	That	student	arrives.
	This	teacher	leaves.
		King	

The { strong man / tallest boy / pretty girl } { laughs. / smiles. / cries. }

He { came to Beijing / went there / arrived home } { yesterday. / last week. / the day before. }

4.3.2 Immediate Constituent Analysis

The structural approach gradually prevailed in the US from the 1920s to the late 1950s. As a pioneer among these structuralists, Leonard Bloomfield put forward Immediate Constituent analysis in his *Language* (1933), attempting to present a structural methodology for the analysis of any language. The Immediate

Constituent analysis (IC analysis) is a method of analyzing a sentence into its immediate component parts. In general, the division is binary, for example, a sentence's immediate constituents are Subject and Predicate. It works in a top—down processing till each word within a sentence.

For Bloomfield, the grammatical forms of a language can be grouped into 3 classes: 1) when a form is spoken alone, it appears in some sentence—type, e.g. *"John!"*. 2) whenever two (or, rarely, more) forms are spoken together, as constituents of a complex form, the grammatical features by which they are combined, make up a construction, for example, the grammatical features by which *poor John* and *ran away* combine in the form *poor John ran away*, make up a construction. 3) a third great class of grammatical forms must probably be set up for the case where a form is spoken as the conventional substitute for any one of a whole class of other forms. Thus, the selective feature by which the form *he* in English is conventional substitute for a whole class of other forms, such as *John, poor John,* and so on, must doubtless be viewed as an example of a third class of grammatical forms, to which we may give the name of substitutions (Bloomfield, 1933: 176–177).

Grammatical Construction refers to any syntactic structure such as a sentence or a phrase. Grammatical constructions within a sentence include any syntactic string of words ranging from sentences, phrasal structures to certain complex lexemes. For example:

Mary ate an apple. (S)

ate an apple (VP)

an apple (NP)

Constituent refers to every linguistic unit, which is a part of a larger linguistic unit in structural sentence analysis. Several constituents together form a construction. For example:

the girl ate the apple. (S) → the girl (NP) + ate the apple (VP)

the girl (NP) → the (determiner) + girl (noun)

ate the apple (VP) → ate (verb) + the apple (noun phrase)

the apple (noun phrase) → the (determiner) + apple (noun)

Immediate Constituent analysis is characterized by a top-down process of analysis. A sentence is seen as a constituent structure with its immediate constituents – word groups (phrases), which are in turn analyzed into the immediate constituents of their own, and the process goes on until the ultimate constituents (word in syntax) are reached. It may be carried out with brackets and shown with tree diagrams as follows.

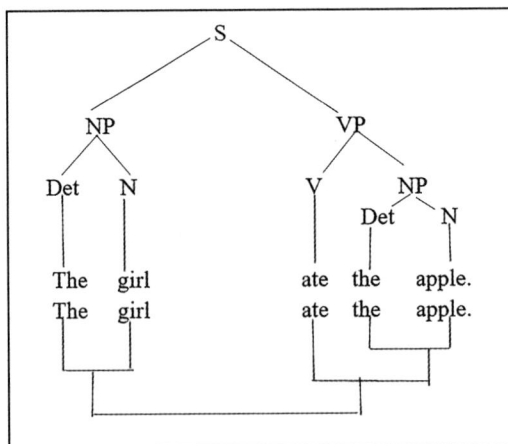

Bracketing is not as common in use, but it is an economic notation in representing the constituent/phrase structure of a grammatical unit. For example:

(((The) (girl)) ((ate) ((the) (apple))))

[S [NP [Det The] [N girl]] [VP [V ate] [NP [Det the] [N apple]]]]

IC analysis can demonstrate the linearity and hierarchy of a sentence, and analyze some structural ambiguities as follows.

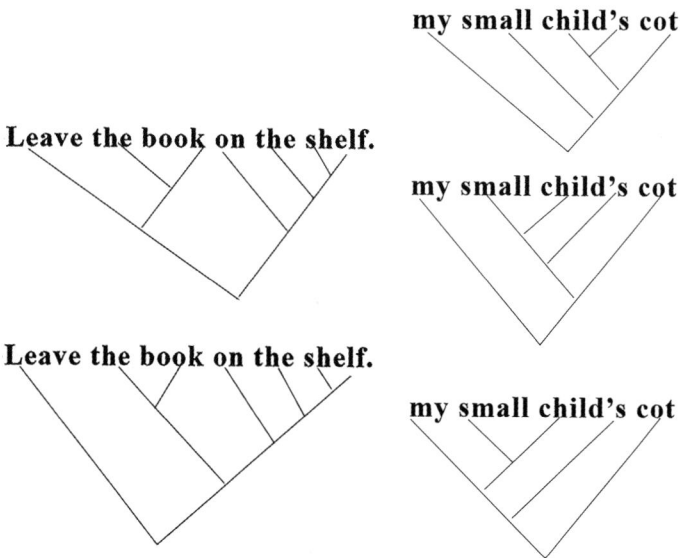

my small child's cot

Leave the book on the shelf.

my small child's cot

Leave the book on the shelf.

my small child's cot

IC analysis can present the different meaning choices of structural ambiguities, but it fails to analyze the syntactic relationship within some expressions like *John is eager to please. & John is easy to please.*

4.3.3 Endocentric and Exocentric Constructions

"Every syntactic construction shows us two (or more) free forms combined in a phrase, which we may call the resultant phrase. The resultant phrase may belong to a form-class other than that of any constituent. For instance, *John ran* is neither a nominative expression (like *John*) nor a finite verb expression (like *ran*). Therefore we say that the English actor-action construction is exocentric: the resultant phrase belongs to the form-class of no immediate constituent. On the other hand, the resultant phrase may belong to the same form-class as one (or more) of the constituents. For instance, *poor John* is a proper-noun expression, and so is the constituent *John*; the forms *John* and *poor John* have, on the whole, the same functions. Accordingly, we say that the English character-substance construction (as in *poor John*, *fresh milk*, and the like) is an endocentric construction" (Bloomfield, 1933: 204).

A grammatical construction (for instance, a phrase or compound) is said to be endocentric if it fulfils the same linguistic function as one of its parts, which serves as the head or center of the whole. An endocentric construction is also known as a headed construction. *Poor John* is functionally equivalent to its head *John*. The two expressions are syntactically the same, and they are substitutable for each other. Typical endocentric constructions include noun phrases, verb phrases, adjective phrases. For example:

the ten most modern cities in the world

will arrive

extremely blue

clean and clear

dark chocolate <u>brown</u>

The head is not necessarily the last constituent. It may occur at the beginning, for example, *faster than a speeding bullet, the newspaper stand at the St. Ives railway station, the man about whom I told you, afraid of the dark, hot beyond endurance.*

Endocentric constructions may be further divided into two subtypes: subordinate and coordinate constructions. Subordinate constructions are endocentric constructions in which there is only one head, with the head being dominant and the other constituents dependent, for example, *beautiful flowers, leave furtively and stealthily, the monkeys in the forest, afraid of the dark.* Coordinate constructions are endocentric constructions in which there are more than one head, and the heads are of equal status which can stand for the original construction functionally. For example, *ladies and gentlemen, clean and clear, the Captain Charlie.* In these expressions both nouns are capable of serving as the head which (each head) can stand for the original construction functionally.

An exocentric construction refers to a group of syntactically related words where none of the words is functionally equivalent to the group as a whole, that is, there is no definable center or head inside the group. The following are typical examples of exocentric constructions:

Basic sentence structures: *John arrived.*

Prepositional phrases: *about whom I told you, beyond endurance*

Verb + Object: *loves Jean*

Verb + Adjective: *looks fine*

4.4 The Transformational-Generative Approach

In the late 1950s, Noam Chomsky (1928–) tried to open up a new route of linguistic study complementing the limitations of the previously-prevailing structural linguistic study of language in America. In 1957, he published the book *Syntactic Structures*. In this book, he proposed Transformational-Generative Grammar (TG grammar) which marked the beginning of the Chomskyan Revolution.

Chomsky begins *Syntactic Structures* by aiming to construct "a grammar that can be viewed as a device of some sort for producing the sentences of the language under analysis. More generally, linguists must be concerned with the problem of determining the fundamental underlying properties of successful grammars. The ultimate outcome of these investigations should be a theory of linguistic structure in which the descriptive devices utilized in particular grammars are presented and studied abstractly, with no specific reference to particular languages. One function of this theory is to provide a general method for selecting a grammar for each language, given a corpus of sentences of this language" (Chomsky, 1957: 11).

TG grammar has undergone three phases of development since 1957. The first phase, from *Syntactic Structure* to *Aspects of the Theory of Syntax*, elaborated the expressive power of grammars to include different levels of representation (*Syntactic Structures*) and a lexicon (the major technical innovation of Chomsky 1965). During this period, Chomsky established the notion of generative grammar, the concepts of phrase structure rules and transformations. The second phase, beginning in the 1960s and culminating in Government and Binding models (1980s), sought to constrain the expressive power of derivations, such operations became very general, along the lines of "Move something", And general principles of the theory of grammar ("Universal Grammar" by the 1960s) constrained such operations to apply appropriately. During the second phase, Chomsky recognized the deep structure and surface structure in sentences, and introduced the semantic component (firstly at the level of deep structure in order to constrain the generation of ill-formed sentences, and then recognized the role of surface structure in semantic interpretation), trace theory, X-Bar Theory, Q-Theory, Case Theory, Binding Theory, and Movement Theory. The third phase has sought substantive economy principles under the Minimalist Program (1995).

In TG grammar, the phrase structure rules generate the basic sentence structures (deep structures), and sentences are formed through transformations into surface structures.

4.4.1 Phrase Structure Rules

Phrases are the immediate constituents of a sentence. In English syntactic analysis, the mostly recognized phrases are noun phrase (NP), verb phrase (VP), adjective phrase (AP) and prepositional phrase (PP). Phrases consist of two levels, i.e., phrase level and word level as exemplified below:

NP: a handsome <u>boy</u> (N)

VP: will <u>arrive</u> (V)

AP: extremely <u>blue</u> (A)

PP: mainly <u>about</u> (P)

A phrase that consists of more than one word usually contains a head, a specifier and a complement. A head is the word around which a phrase is formed. The constituent on the left side of the head is a specifier. The constituent on the right side of the head is a complement. In English syntax, a certain word can only concur with certain other words. There must be certain grammatical mechanism ensuring the appropriate constituents for specifiers, heads, and complements in phrase structure. The grammatical mechanism that regulates the arrangement of elements that constitute a phrase is called a phrase structure rule. The phrase structure rules for NP, VP, AP, and PP can be written as follows:

NP $\rightarrow$ (Det) N (PP)$\cdots$

VP $\rightarrow$ (Qual) V (NP) $\cdots$

AP $\rightarrow$ (Deg) A (PP) $\cdots$

PP $\rightarrow$ (Deg) P (NP) $\cdots$

The arrow can be read as "consist of" or "branches into". The parenthesis means the inside element can be omitted and the three dots mean other complement options are available. A NP can consist of a determiner, a N head, and a PP complement. A VP can be formed with a qualifier, a V, and a NP complement. An AP can be composed of a degree word, an A, and a PP complement. As illustrated above, a phrase can be just a head with specifiers and complements both optional.

4.4.1.1 XP Rule

From the above four types of English phrases, we find structural similarities for a single phrase structure.

the XP rule: XP → (specifier) X (complement)

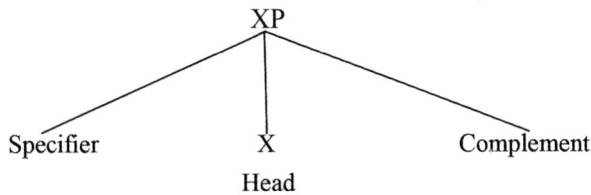

4.4.1.2 X- Theory

In complex phrases like *government decision to open schools*, the noun phrase *decision to open schools* is an immediate level or category larger than the head but smaller than the full XP. Such intermediate level formed by the head and the complement between word level and phrase level is represented by the symbol X- (pronounced as X bar). Thus the XP structure rule turns to two-phrase structure rules:

a.XP → (Specifier) X-

b.X- → X (Complement)

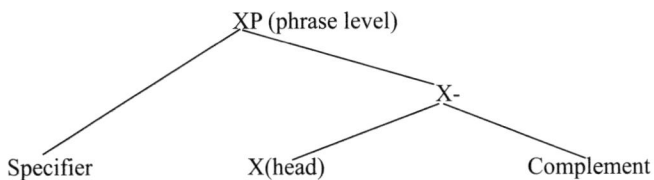

The first rule indicates that XP categories such as NP and VP consist of an optional specifier (a determiner, a qualifier, and so on) and an X–. The second rule states that an X– consists of a head, X, and any complements.

4.4.1.3 Coordination Rule

Besides subordinate phrases illustrated above, there are coordinate phrases in headed structures. Such coordinate phrases are called coordinate structures. And this phenomenon is called coordination. Coordination can occur at any level (a head or an entire XP), and consists of unlimited number of coordinated categories. The category type of the coordinate phrase is identical to the category type of the elements being conjoined. The coordination rule runs as:

$$X \rightarrow X * Con\ X$$

The symbol X stands for a category at any structural level, and can be either an X or XP that is coordinated. The asterisk (*) indicates that one or more categories can occur to the left of the Con (conjunction).

Phrase structure rules (PS rules) are also called rewrite rules or categorical rules.

4.4.2 Phrase Elements

As is illustrated in 4.4.1, a phrase can consist of specifiers and complements besides the head. In this section, we will introduce the elements of a phrase to accommodate the more complex phrase structures.

XP	Specifier	Head	Complement
NP	government	decision	to open schools
NP		fact/ belief/ claim	that she would go abroad next month
VP	both	speak	French
VP		hope/ believe/ suggest	that the boy would go home
AP	merely	anxious	to get on his way
AP		afraid/ certain/ aware	that nobody would believe me
PP	about	whom	I told you
PP		over/ about	whether it is better to keep trying

Examples of English Phrases

4.4.2.1 Specifiers

In phrase structure rule, specifiers have both special semantic and syntactic roles. Semantically, they help make more precise the meaning of the head. Syntactically, they typically mark a phrase boundary. They mark the beginning of phrases. They are attached to the top level of a phrase structures, to the left of the head. For example, determiners serve as the specifiers of Ns, qualifiers typically function as the specifiers of Vs, and degree word as the specifiers of As and sometimes Ps.

4.4.2.2 Complements

Complements are optional elements in a phrase. They themselves can be a phrase or a clause and provide detailed information for the head. They are attached to the right of the head in English, for example, *a story about a sports champion, I believe that you will win.*

The information about the complement is included in the head and termed subcategorization. Subcategorization information together with the phrase structure rules ensures that lexical items appear in the appropriate types of tree structures. A certain lexical item requires a certain type of complement. For example, intransitive verbs like *arrive/ appear* can occur without any complement; some transitive verbs like *cut/ love/ use* can occur with a NP complement; and some transitive verbs like *give/ put* can take more than one complement. Therefore, we revise our original XP rule as follows, using asterisk after the complement to indicate that one or more is permitted.

The XP Rule (revise)

XP → (Specifier) X (Complement *)

It is noted that complements in English occur to the right of the head, which is in contrast with the Chinese equivalent. Words which introduce the sentence complement are termed complementizers (shortened as Cs). The sentence introduced by the complementizer is called a complement clause, for example, *I believe that you will win.* The complement clause is termed a complement phrase (CP) in the whole sentence which is called a matrix clause. A matrix clause is a construction in which the complement phrase is embedded. There is no limit on the number of embedded clauses that can occur in an English sentence.

4.4.2.3 Modifiers

Modifiers indicate specific properties of heads. They are optional elements in phrase structures. In English, modifiers can occur either to the left side of the head or to the right side, for example, *a very tempting choice, dark chocolate brown, the highly emotive actor, walk with caution, speak fast*. Therefore we revise our earlier XP rule to allow the various options of modifiers.

The Extended XP rule:

XP → (Spec) (Mod) X (Complement *) (Mod)

4.4.3 Sentences

In TG grammar, sentences also have their own heads like other phrases. A sentence takes an abstract category inflection (dubbed "Infl") as its head, which indicates the sentence's tense and agreement. A sentence takes a NP (the subject) as its specifier and a VP category as its complement. Thus sentences have the same internal structure as phrases and are consistent with the XP rule outlined earlier. Actually, XP rule makes a universal endocentric phrase model through complement's dependency on a head. It is noted that TG grammar is different from Bloomfield's IC analysis, especially in the point of describing sentences as conforming to the universal endocentric phrase model. The structure of S can be outlined as follows.

Infl P (= S)

NP Infl VP

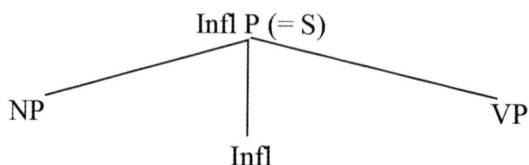

Inflection position can be taken by an abstract category encoded in a verb which indicates the sentence's tense or an auxiliary as shown below.

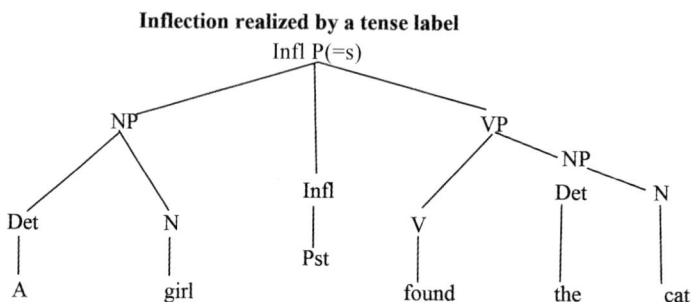

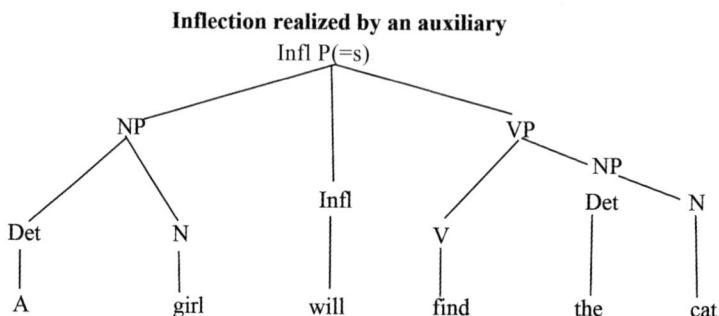

Inflection realized by a tense label

Infl P(=s)

NP Infl VP

Det N V NP

A girl Pst found Det N

the cat

Inflection realized by an auxiliary

Infl P(=s)

NP Infl VP

Det N V NP

A girl will find Det N

the cat

4.4.4 Transformations

The phrase structure rules have provided mechanisms explaining how different phrases are formed and how a simple declarative sentence takes inflection as its head and NP as its specifier and VP as its complement. How about other sentence types such as interrogative, imperative and exclamatory? In this section, we will explain some of these phenomena.

4.4.4.1 Auxiliary Movement

According to the phrase structure rules, the auxiliary is the head of a sentence which takes NP, the subject, as its specifier on the left and a VP category as its complement on the right. Yes−no questions take the following two steps to change the position of its auxiliary: In the first step, the usual XP rule is used to form a structure in which the auxiliary occupies its normal position in Infl, between the subject and the VP. In the second step, transformation which is a special type of rule that can move an element from one position to another will move the auxiliary from the Infl position to a position to the left of the subject. This type of transformation is called inversion.

Inversion: Move Infl to the left of the subject NP.

What position does the auxiliary move into in the XP rule? The position the auxiliary occupies is the same as the position that a complementizer occupies. All sentences can occur within larger Complementizer Phrases (CPs), whether they are embedded or not. In yes− no question the Infl is moved to the complementizer (C) position which is empty as follows.

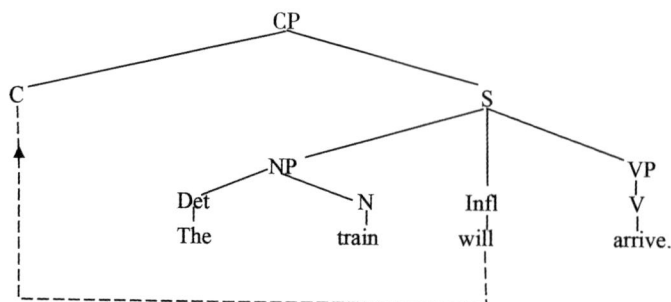

Inversion (revised): Move Infl to C.

If the CP is embedded in a larger sentence or matrix clause, it can contain an overt complementizer such as "that" or "whether" in the C position. There can be only one element in each position in a tree structure which means complementizers and auxiliaries are mutually exclusive. So in a CP, we would find that a clause can be introduced by either a complementizer or an inverted auxiliary, but not the two at the same time. For example, *I wonder whether it will rain tomorrow.*

A transformation can change the position of an element in a sentence. But it does not change its category and can not eliminate any part of the structural configuration created by the phrase structure rules. Thus, the original position of "will" remains empty which is marked by the symbol *e* ("empty") and called a trace. It records the fact that the moved element comes from the head position within the sentence.

The auxiliary moves from the head Infl position in Inflection phrase into the head C position in CP. The auxiliary inversion involves the movement of a word from the head position in one phrase into the head position in another. Such a movement is called head movement.

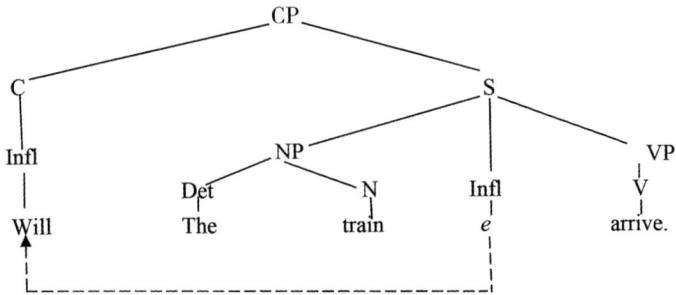

4.4.4.2 Do Insertion

Sentences such as "*I care.*" does not have an overt inflection form. In transforming this type of sentences into a yes-no question, we need to add the auxiliary verb *do*.

Do insertion: Insert interrogative *do* into an empty Infl position.

After the auxiliary *do* is inserted into the Infl position, we can make the inversion of *do* to the C position to form a yes-no question.

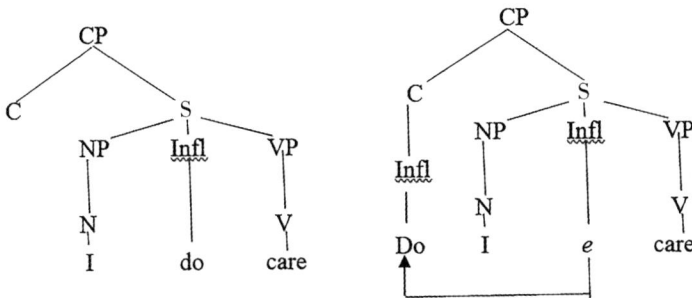

Do insertion   Do inversion

4.4.4.3 Deep Structure and Surface Structure

The preceding examples show how the mechanisms of XP rule and transformations work: the XP rule determines the internal structure of phrasal categories, and transformations change the form of the sentence by moving an element from one position to another in the tree diagram. The abstract representation of the syntactic properties of a construction is called deep structure of a sentence i.e., the underlying level of structural relations between its different constituents, such as the relation between the underlying subject and its verb, or a verb and its object. The final stage in syntactic derivation of a construction is called surface structure of a sentence, which closely corresponds to the structural organization of a construction people actually produce and receive.

4.4.4.4 **Wh**-Movement

How do Wh-questions come about? What is their deep structure? To get the answer, we had better understand the role of the Wh-words before the auxiliary.

What do you want?

Which dress do you prefer?

It seems clear that the bold words in each sentence function as the complement of the verb. The deep structures of the above sentences are:

you want what

you prefer which dress

To convert these deep structures into the corresponding surface structures, we need a transformation that moves the Wh–phrase from its position in deep structure to a position at the beginning of the sentence. This transformation is called Wh–Movement. As the whole sentence is a CP and the moved auxiliary is located originally in the C position. It is moved to the specifier position of the CP.

Wh–Movement: Move the Wh–phrase to the specifier position under CP

As for wh–subject questions like *Who opened the door?*, Wh–phrase originally functions as a subject. When it moves to the specifier position within the CP, the actual word order of the sentence does not change. This movement can be shown as follows.

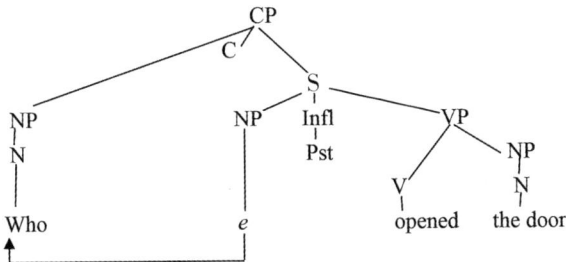

4.5 The Functional Approach

In contrast with formal linguistics which puts emphasis on analysis of language forms; functional linguistics states that our communicative meaning determines our choice of language forms. As mentioned in Chapter One, Functional linguistics comprises of several linguistic schools. Concerning sentences, we mainly introduce THEME and RHEME, Systemic–Functional grammar and cohesions in English.

4.5.1 Theme and Rheme

Theme–Rheme analysis is put forward by Mathesius (1882–1945) and developed by M.A.K. Halliday. Mathesius holds that theme is the basis or the starting point of the utterance that is known or at least obvious in the given situation and from which the speaker proceeds. And rheme is the nucleus or the core of the utterance. It is what the speaker states about, or in regard to the starting point of the utterance. Halliday distinguished "Given + New" and "Theme + Rheme" in stating "There is a close semantic relationship between information structure and thematic structure. Other things being equal, a speaker will choose the Theme from within what is Given and locate the focus, the climax of the New, somewhere in the Rheme". But "Theme + Rheme is speaker–oriented, while Given + New is listener–oriented. But both are speaker–selected" (Halliday, 1994: 299).

Halliday identifies English Theme as the initial element of the clause and defines theme functionally in structural configuration with the Rheme. Theme and rheme organizes the clause as a message. Within that configuration, "the Theme is the starting–point for the message; it is the ground from which the clause is taking off" (Halliday, 1994: 38). Rheme is the nucleus or the core of the utterance. It is what the speaker states about, or in regard to the starting point of the utterance. It is natural for speakers to start from the known to the unknown, and the theme–rheme order is the usual one in unemotional narration, which is called objective order. In emotional narration, it may be possible to reverse the order. And this is a subjective order. So part of the meaning of any clause lies in which element is chosen as its theme (Halliday, 1994: 38). For example:

1)*My mother* did the work on Tuesday.

2)*The work* was done on Tuesday by my mother.

3)*On Tuesday,* my mother did the work.

In the first sentence, the theme is *my mother* which is also the subject of the verb. The sentence is natural and unmarked. In the second sentence, the theme is *the work* which is a grammatical subject in passive voice. *The work* as the patient of the verb is emphasized. The sentence is marked. In the third sentence, the theme is *on Tuesday*, which is not the grammatical subject of the sentence. It is raised to the beginning of the sentence to mark for emphasis. Besides, the theme of a clause can also be marked off in speech by intonation (Halliday, 1994: 39).

The flow of information in a sentence from Theme to Rheme is crucial in achieving communicative effectiveness of a message. The exchange of information between successive Theme and Rheme pairings in a text is called Thematic Progression (Eggins, 1994). Thematic progression contributes to the cohesive development of a text, that is to say, in a cohesive text the distribution of given and new information needs to follow certain patterns. There are mainly four types of Thematic Progression in English and French (Xu, 2010:160) as follows.

Type 1:

Theme 1 → rheme 1

Theme 1 → rheme 2

Theme 1 → rheme 3

Type 3:

Theme 1 → rheme 1

Theme 2 → rheme 1

Theme 3 → rheme 1

Type 2:

Theme 1 → rheme 1

Theme 2 → rheme 2   Theme 2 → rheme 3   Theme 2 → rheme4

Type 4:

Theme 1 → rheme 1

Theme 2 → rheme 2

Theme 3 → rheme 3

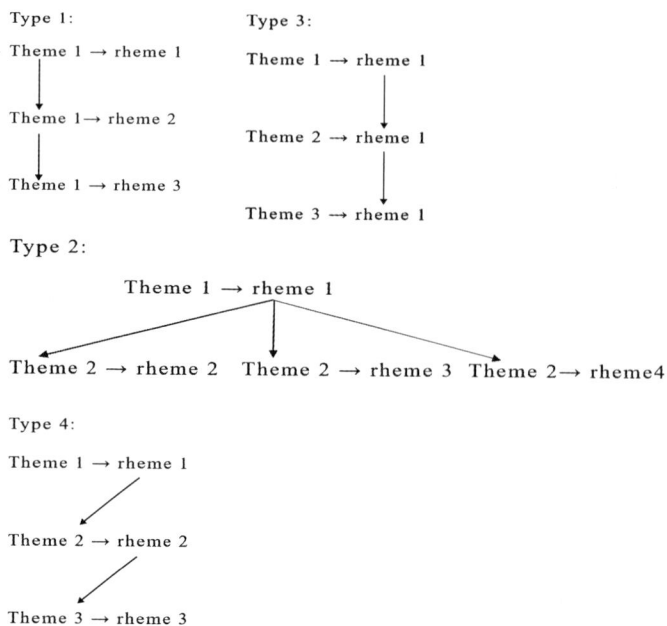

4.5.2 Systemic-Functional Grammar

Systemic-Functional grammar has two components: Systemic grammar and Functional grammar. The systemic part means language elements form into systems. The use of language involves a network of systems of meaning potentials. The items in a system are in a choice relation with each other. Meaning determines the choice of language form, not vice versa. Meaning is realized through form. The goal of Systemic-Functional grammar is to see how function and meaning are realized through forms. It is in contrast with formal linguistics which emphasizes the syntactic structure of language. Halliday has inherited the idea that language is a social phenomenon and emphasizes the study of language in relation to the functions it performs. He puts forward the three metafunctions of language, i.e., ideational, interpersonal and textual functions, which are related to three grammatical systems respectively: transitivity, mood and theme.

"It is functional in the sense that it is designed to account for how the language is used. Every text—that is, everything that is said or written—unfolds in some context of use; furthermore, it is the uses of language that, over tens of thousands of generations, have shaped the system. Language has evolved to satisfy human needs; and the way it is organized is functional with respect to these needs—it is not arbitrary. A functional grammar is essentially a 'natural' grammar, in the sense that everything in it can be explained, ultimately, by reference to how language is used. Following from this, the fundamental components of meaning in language are functional components. All languages are organized around two main kinds of meaning, the 'ideational' or reflective, and the 'interpersonal' or active. These components, called 'metafunctions' in the terminology of the present theory, are the manifestations in the linguistic system of the two very general purposes which underlie all uses of language: (i) to understand the environment (ideational), and (ii) to act on the others in it (interpersonal). Combined with these is a third metafunctional component, the 'textual', which breathes relevance into the other two. (Halliday 1994: F39).

Commodity exchanged / Role in exchange	Goods/ services	Information
Giving	Offer Would you like this teapot?	Statement He's giving her the teapot.
Demanding	Command Give me that teapot!	Question What is he giving her?

(Halliday 1994: 69)

According to the commodities exchanged in language communication, Halliday defines the four primary speech functions of offer, command, statement and question. And speakers play roles of giving or demanding in interpersonal communication.

Functionally, sentences can be classified into the following types.

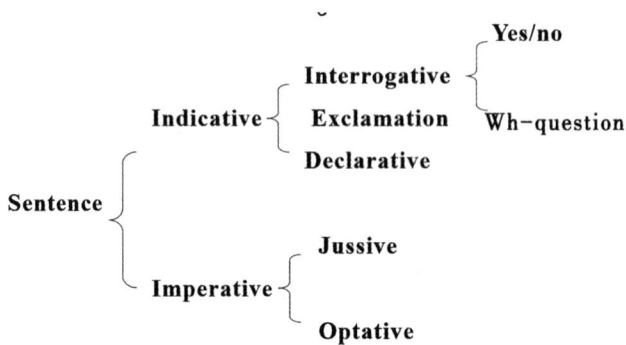

```
                                          ┌ Yes/no
                         ┌ Interrogative ┤
         ┌ Indicative ┤   Exclamation   └ Wh-question
         │              └ Declarative
Sentence ┤
         │              ┌ Jussive
         └ Imperative ┤
                        └ Optative
```

4.5.3 Cohesion in English

Cohesion in English (Halliday &Hasan, 2001) presents a grammar between sentences in a text. A text is a unit of language in use. A text is a semantic unit: a unit not of form but of meaning. A text does not consist of sentences; it is realized by sentences through cohesion. Cohesion refers to relations of meaning that exist within the text, especially those surface-structure features which link different elements and define it as a text. The wholeness of meaning of the text is called coherence. There are grammatical and lexical cohesions. Grammatical cohesion is realized by reference, substitution, ellipsis, and conjunction. Lexical cohesion is realized by reiteration and collocation. For example:

1) Anaphoric Reference (a word in a text refers back to other ideas in the text for its meaning.): for example, I went out with Jean on Sunday. She looked awful.

2) Cataphoric reference (a word in a text refers to another later in the text.): e.g. When he arrived, John noticed that the door was open.

3) Exophoric reference (a word refers to an idea outside the text. This is a reference to world knowledge shared by the reader.): E.g. The Prime Minister responded quickly to the threat.

4) Substitution: for example, Now we're finishing our essays. I know you want to go out, but before you can do that, please finish.

5) Ellipsis: e.g. I have checked my result online. Have you?

6) Conjunction: e.g. In addition to giving up meat, I also stopped eating dairy products.

7) Reiteration/ repetition: for example, The problem with contemporary art is that it is not easily understood by most people. Contemporary art is deliberately abstract, and that means it leaves the viewer wondering what she is looking at.

8) Collocation: (Halliday defines collocation as the tendency of certain lexical items to co-occur.) for example,

There was a fat man of Bombay,

Who was <u>smoking</u> one sunshiny day,

When a bird called a snipe,

Flew away with his <u>pipe</u>,

Which vexed the fat man of Bombay.

(https://americanliterature.com/author/mother-goose/nursery-rhyme/ there-was-a-fat-man-of-bombay)

Further Readings:

Bloomfield, Leonard. 2002. *Language*. Beijing: Foreign Language Teaching and Research Press.

Cook, V. 2000. *Chomsky's Universal Grammar 2nd Edition*. Beijing: Foreign Language Teaching and Research Press.

Halliday, M. A. K. 2000. *An Introduction to Functional Grammar 2nd Edition*. Beijing: Foreign Language Teaching and Research Press.

Halliday, M. A. K. & Hasan, R. 1976/2001. *Cohesion in English*. 北京:外语教学与研究出版社.

Thompson, A. et al. 2000. *Introducing Functional Grammar 2nd Edition*. Beijing: Foreign Language Teaching and Research Press.

胡壮麟、朱永生、张德禄、李战子,2005,《系统功能语言学概论》. 北京:北京大学出版社.

石定栩, 2002,《乔姆斯基的形式句法》. 北京 : 北京语言大学出版社 .

Questions and Exercises:

1.Define the following terms:

syntax, category, sentence, syntagmatic relations, paradigmatic relations, endocentric constructions, exocentric constructions, coordination, subordination, construction, constituent, IC analysis, deep structure, surface structure, phrase structure rules, transformational rules, X−bar, the six cohesive devices

2.How is sentence defined?

3.What contributions did traditional grammar make to modern linguistics?

4.Use your own examples to illustrate the linear structure and hierarchical structure of sentence.

5.Try to analyze the following paragraph through thematic progression, and draw a picture to describe that are talked in the passage.

Perhaps the most unforgettable thing in the bazaar, apart from its general atmosphere, is the place where they make linseed oil. It is a vast, somber cavern of a room, some thirty feet high and sixty feet square, and so thick with the dust of centuries that the mudbrick walls and vaulted roof are only dimly visible. In this cavern are three massive stone wheels, each with a huge pole through its centre as an axle. The pole is attached at the one end to an upright post, around which it can revolve, and at the other to a blind-folded camel, which walks constantly in a circle, providing the motive power to turn the stone wheel. This revolves in a circular stone channel, into which an attendant feeds linseed (excerpt from "The Middle Eastern Bazaar", Advanced English, FLTRP).

Chapter 5

Semantics: The Meaning of Language

语 言 学 导 论
新文科思政教程

5.1 Introduction

As informative function of language is its primary function and a prerequisite of social development, the meaning of language is a focus in linguistic studies. From a systematic point of view, language is of different levels, with corresponding linguistic branches of phonology, syntax, and semantics. There are correlations between these branches. Leech (1981: 11) points out that for the analysis of any sentence, we need to establish a phonological representation, a syntactic representation and a semantic representation, and the stages by which one level of representation can be derived from another as in the following chart.

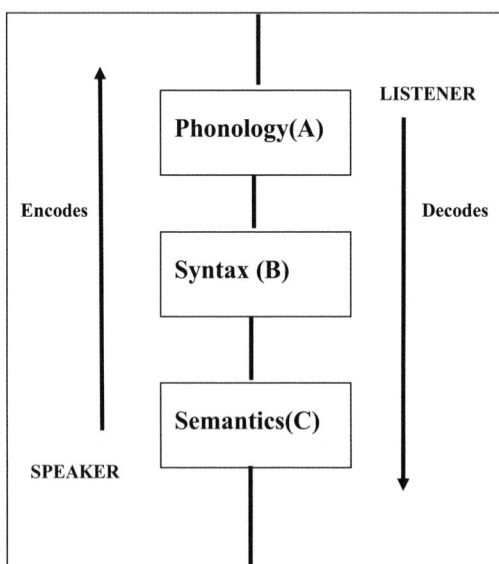

In philosophy, the relationship between linguistic expressions and their meanings is an everlasting topic which can be traced back to Plato's naming theory in *Cratylus*, and Aristotle's conventional view in *On Interpretation* (Wang, 2011:1). According to German philosopher Frege (8 November 1848–26 July 1925), who is widely considered to be the greatest logician since Aristotle, each linguistic expression may have two types of meaning, i.e. sense and reference. The reference (or referent) of a proper name is the object it means or indicates, whereas its sense is what the name expresses. The reference of a sentence is its truth value, whereas its sense is the thought that it expresses.

The term *Semantics* comes from the book "Essai de Sémantique"(1897) written by French linguist Michel Bréal, who is often identified as a founder of modern semantics. As a subbranch of linguistics, semantics is the study of meaning, more specifically, it is the study of the meaning of linguistic units, words and sentences in particular. This chapter mainly talks about the study of meaning, word meaning, sentence meaning, and semantic analysis.

Learning Objectives:

1. Remember the following terms: the semantic triangle, conceptual meaning, Leech's seven types of meaning, reference, sense, synonymy, antonymy, hyponymy, meronymy, polysemy, homonymy, semantic field, entailment, presupposition, componential analysis, predication analysis, proposition

2. Understand: What are the different approaches to meaning?

   What are the basic sense relations?

What is componential analysis?

3. Illustrate with examples: The sense relations of words /sentences

The different kinds of antonyms/ synonyms

The sense relations and corresponding figures of speech

Componential analysis

4. Tell examples: Typical sense of relations of words in Chinese language

Lead-in Questions:

1. What do terms "connotation, denotation" mean? E.g. 社会主义核心价值观的内涵 . And find more examples for illustration.

2. Find differences of sense relations of words between Chinese and English, for example, "知否，知否，应是绿肥红瘦"，Chinese equivalent expressions of "uncle".

5.2 Traditional Study of Meaning in China

作为一种表意语言，古代中国语言文字学肇始于对"字"义的解释和归类的小学，如《尔雅》。自秦朝统一后，中国封建社会崇尚传统典籍的微言大义，经书训释成为秦汉时期的社会需要，小学附庸于经学。作为中国传统语言学的小学，通常分为三个部分：文字学（《说文》类）、音韵类（《切韵》类）和训诂类（《尔雅》和经传类）。除了这三门还应当包括比较词汇学（《方言》类）、词源学（《释名》类）和虚字类（《语助》类）。训诂学专门研究语义和句法格式，文字学研究字的本义、常用义和假借义，比较词汇学研究不同方言词汇的词义，词源学研究词的语源和词族，虚字研究虚字的功能语义。其中，训诂学可以说是汉语经典语义学的主体。中国古典语义学为现代汉语语义学研究奠定了深厚的基础，如按义类分析汉语实词、运用文献语言推求词义中的义素等，尤其是《说文》是一部完整的古老的某一语言的语义系统（对象的系统性和方法的系统性的一致）的专著（王晓斌，2004）。

《尔雅》是中国第一部词典，收录4300多个词语，按义类编排，计2091个条目，旨在提供语音、词汇和语法等方面都合乎规范的标准语。《尔雅》被认为是中国训诂的开山之作，是我国第一部按义类编排的综合性辞书，这些条目按类别分为"释诂""释言"、"释训"、"释亲"、"释宫"、"释器"、"释乐"、"释天"、"释地"、"释丘"、"释山"、"释水"、"释草"、"释木"、"释虫"、"释鱼"、"释鸟"、"释兽"、"释畜"等19篇。

谓女子，先生为姊，后生为妹。——《尔雅·释亲》

春为发生，夏为长嬴，秋为收成，冬为安宁。——《尔雅·释天》

比翼双飞："南方有比翼鸟焉，不比不飞，其名谓之鹣鹣。"——《尔雅·释地》（https://www.guoxuebaike.cn/20210415/erya/）

5.3 Approaches to Meaning

From 1897 to the 1960s, it witnessed several linguists' views on meaning such as Bloomfield's behaviorist view of meaning, Ogden and Richards' conceptualst view of meaning, Trier's Theory of Semantic Field, componential analysis and predication analysis. From the 1960s onward, semantics has enjoyed a diversified development trend.

5.3.1 Naming View

According to the naming view, represented by Plato, language expressions stand naturally for the things they refer to in the real world.

The formal topic of the *Cratylus* is "correctness of names", a hot topic in the late fifth century BC when the dialogue has its dramatic setting. Sophists like Prodicus offered training courses in this subject, sometimes perhaps meaning by it little more than lessons in correct diction. But that practical issue spawned the theoretical question, what criteria determine the correct choice of name for any given object? And in the *Cratylus* Socrates' two primary interlocutors, Hermogenes and Cratylus (the latter of whom is reported by Aristotle to have been an early philosophical influence on Plato), represent two diametrically opposed answers to that question.

As a preliminary, it is important to be clear about what is meant by "names". The plural noun onomata (singular onoma), translated "names", in fact varies between being (a) a general term for "words", (b) more narrowly, nouns, or perhaps nouns and adjectives, and (c) in certain contexts, proper names alone. In (a), the most generic use, it comes to designate language as such. Ultimately, for this reason, the *Cratylus* is Plato's dialogue about language, even if the elements of language on which it concentrates are in fact mainly nouns. Proper names are included among these nouns, and at times are treated as paradigmatic examples of them. The positions of Hermogenes and Cratylus have come to be known to modern scholarship as "conventionalism" and "naturalism" respectively.

An extreme linguistic conventionalist like Hermogenes holds that nothing but local or national convention determines which words are used to designate which objects. The same names could have been attached to quite different objects, and the same objects given quite different names, so long as the users of the language were party to the convention. Cratylus, as an extreme linguistic naturalist, holds that names cannot be arbitrarily chosen in the way that conventionalism describes or advocates, because names belong naturally to their specific objects. If you try to speak of something with any name other than its natural name, you are simply failing to refer to it at all. For example, he has told Hermogenes to the latter's intense annoyance, Hermogenes is not actually his name.

Socrates is the main speaker in this dialogue, and his arguments are generally taken to represent Plato's own current views. He starts out by criticizing conventionalism, and persuades Hermogenes that some kind of naturalism must be endorsed. This leads to a long central section in which Socrates' version of naturalism is spelt out by appeal to proposed etymologies of philosophically important words: those words, it turns out, have not been attached in a merely arbitrary way to their objects, but are encoded descriptions of them. So far the argument seems to be going Cratylus' way. But in the final part of the dialogue Socrates turns to Cratylus and shows him that his expectations as a naturalist are set impossibly high: names cannot aspire to being perfect encapsulations of their objects' essences, and some element of convention must be conceded (https://plato.stanford.edu/entries/plato-cratylus/) .

The limitation of naming view is that it is confined to nouns only, and it is difficult to extend this naming view to include other parts of speech. And some abstract nouns such as logic, beauty, imagination, courage, love and hatred do not refer to objects in the world at all.

5.3.2 Conceptualist View

Different from the naming view which relates words and things directly, conceptualism holds that words and the things they refer to are related through mediation of concepts in the mind, as illustrated by the semantic triangle charted in Ogden and Richard's book "The Meaning of Meaning" in 1923. SYMBOL refers to the language expressions (word, sentence, etc.), REFERENT refers to the thing in the world of experience, and THOUGHT refers to the concept. The relation between the symbol and the referent is not direct but by way of the thought/ reference, the concept in the mind of the speaker.

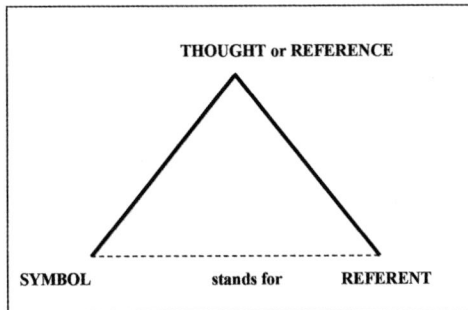

Between a thought and a symbol causal relations hold. When we speak, the symbolism we employ is caused partly by the reference we are making and partly by social and psychological factors—the purpose for which we are making the reference, the proposed effect of our symbols on other persons, and our own attitude. When we hear what is said, the symbols both cause us to perform an act of reference and to assume an attitude which will, according to circumstances, be more or less similar to the act and the attitude of the speaker.

Between the Thought and the Referent there is also a relation; more or less direct (as when we think about or attend to a colored surface we see), or indirect (as when we 'think of' or 'refer to' Napoleon), in which case there may be a very long chain of sign–situations intervening between the act and its referent: word–*historian*–contemporary record–eye–witness–referent (*Napoleon*).

Between the symbol and the referent there is no relevant relation other than the indirect one, which consists in its being used by someone to stand for a referent. Symbol and Referent, that is to say, are not connected directly (and when, for grammatical reasons, we imply such a relation, it will merely be an imputed, as opposed to a real, relation) but only indirectly round the two sides of the triangle (Ogden & Richards, 1923: 10–12).

5.3.3 Behavioristic View

Bloomfield presents a behavioristic view of meaning in his *Language* (1933: 145–150): we have defined the meaning of a linguistic form as the situation in which the speaker utters it and the response which it calls forth in the hearer. ⋯ In practice, we define the meaning of a linguistic form, wherever we can, in terms of some other science. Where this is impossible, we resort to makeshift devices. One is demonstration. If someone did not know the meaning of the word *apple*, we could instruct him by handing him an apple, and continuing, as long as he made mistakes, to handle apples and point at them, until he used the word in the conventional way. This is essentially the process by which children learn the use of speech-forms. ⋯ Adherents of mentalistic psychology believe that they can avoid the difficulty of defining meanings, because they believe that, prior to the utterance of a linguistic form, there occurs within the speaker a non-physical process, a thought, concept, image, feeling, act of will, or the like, and that the hearer, likewise, upon receiving the sound-waves, goes through an equivalent or correlated mental process. The mentalist, therefore, can define the meaning of a linguistic form as the characteristic mental event which occurs in every speaker and hearer in connection with the utterance or hearing of the linguistic form. ⋯ In sum, then, the "mental processes" seem to the mechanist to be merely traditional names for bodily processes which either (1) come within the definition of meaning as speaker's situation, or (2) are so distantly correlated with speech-utterance as to be negligible factors in the speaker's situation, or (3) are mere reproductions of the speech-utterance. ⋯ In practice, then, all linguists, both mentalists and mechanists, define meanings in terms of the speaker's situation and, whenever this seems to add anything, of the hearer's response.

5.3.4 Contextual View

Functional linguists, represented by London School, sees the meaning of language from its use in specific contexts. Context is generally considered as constituted by the knowledge shared by the speaker and hearer. Various components of shared knowledge have been identified, e.g. knowledge of the language they use, knowledge of what has been said before, knowledge about the world in general, knowledge about the specific situation in which linguistic communication is taking place, and knowledge about each other (Dai, 2002: 86). There is a typical case: "A: Do you want some coffee? B: Coffee would keep me awake." In this case, there is a default of "Yes"/ "No" in B's answer, which gives rise to contradictory implications. And this uncertainty can be solved only when the contexts are definite.

5.4 Word Meaning

Concerning word meaning, we are concerned with the meanings of words and the relations between the meanings of words. The meanings of words can be classified into different types such as sense and reference, the seven types of meaning and semantic field.

5.4.1 Sense and Reference

Sense and reference are two related but different aspects of word meaning. Sense refers to the main features, the defining properties an entity has, e.g. the sense of desk is a piece of furniture with a flap top and four legs, at which one reads and writes. Sense is equivalent to concept. The concept of desk may also be called the sense of desk. Sense presents the way people relate words to each other within the framework of their language. Reference is the concrete entities having these properties (e.g. a particular desk in the world), what a linguistic form refers to in the real physical world. Reference deals with the relationship between linguistic elements and the non–linguistic world of experience. Every word has a sense, i.e. some conceptual content; but not every word has a reference. Grammatical words like *but, if, and* do not refer to anything. Words like *unicorn, Santa Claus, God, ghost, fairy, demon* and *dragon* refer to imaginary things, which do not exist in reality. Abstract words like sincerity, love don't have a concrete referent in the world. Linguistic forms having the same sense may have different references in different situations; on the other hand, there are also occasions, when linguistic forms with the same reference might differ in sense, e.g. Frege's statements: "The morning star is the evening star" and "The morning star is the morning star".

If we found, in general, "a=a" and "a=b" to have different cognitive values, the explanation is that for the cognitive value of the sentence, its sense, namely the thought it expresses, is no less relevant than its reference, that is its truth–value. If a=b, the reference of "b" is the same as "a" and therefore the truth–value of "a=a" is the same as that of "a=b". in spite of this, the sense of "b" may differ from that of "a", and thereby the thought expressed in "a=b" may differ from the one expressed in "a=a". in this case the two sentences don't have the same cognitive value. If we understand by "judgement" the advance from the thought to its truth-value, as in the above paper, we can also say that the judgements are different (Textor, 2011: 114).

As analyzed by Frege, reference does help prove the truth-value of a proposition. While, on the other side, sense, which is equivalent to the conceptual meaning of words, is an indispensable part of word meaning and sentence meaning. When reference counts little, sense may count in the truth value of a sentence (Saeed, 2009: 87–111).

5.4.2 Seven Types of Meaning

In his book "Semantics: The Study of Meaning", Geoffrey Leech proposes seven types of meaning: "I shall break down 'meaning' in its widest sense into seven different ingredients, giving primary importance to logical meaning or (as I shall prefer to call it) CONCEPTUAL MEANING, the type of meaning I was discussing earlier in connection with 'semantic competence'. The six other types I shall consider are connotative meaning, social meaning, affective meaning, reflected meaning, collocative meaning and thematic meaning" (Leech, 1981: 9). Leech places connotative meaning, social meaning, affective meaning, reflected meaning and collocative meaning under the type of "associative meaning"(Leech, 1981: 23).

SEVEN TYPES OF MEANING

1.CONCEPTUAL MEANING or Sense		Logical, cognitive, or denotative content.
ASSOCIATIVE MEANING	2.CONNOTATIVE MEANING	What is communicated by virtue of what language refers to.
	3.SOCIAL MEANING	What is communicated of the social circumstances of language use.
	4.AFFECTIVE MEANING	What is communicated of the feelings and attitudes of the speaker/ writer.
	5.REFLECTED MEANING	What is communicated through association with another sense of the same expression.
	6.COLLOCATIVE MEANING	What is communicated through association with words which tend to occur in the environment of another word.
7.THEMATIC MEANING		What is communicated by the way in which the message is organized in terms of order and emphasis.

Conceptual meaning (sometimes called "denotative" or "cognitive" meaning) is widely assumed to be the central factor in linguistic communication, and it can be shown to be integral to the essential function of language in a way that other types of meaning are not (Leech, 1981: 9). It is defined as the logical, cognitive, or denotative content. In other words, it overlaps to a large extent with the notion of reference. But Leech also analyzes conceptual meaning by componential analysis, paradigmatic and syntagmatic axes of linguistic structure in the three-layer of any sentence (a phonological representation, a syntactic representation and a semantic representation). He uses "sense" as a briefer term for his conceptual meaning. As a result, Leech's conceptual meaning has two sides: sense and reference. Conceptual meaning is constant and relatively stable. It forms the basis for linguistic communication because the same word has the same conceptual meaning to all speakers of the same language.

Connotative meaning is the communicative value an expression has by virtue of what it refers to, over and above its purely conceptual content. For example, the conceptual meaning of *woman* includes its reference and the three criteria properties of "human", "adult" and "female". But there is a multitude of additional, non-criterial properties that we expect a referent of woman to possess. They include not only physical characteristics ("biped", "having a womb"), but also psychological and social properties ("gregarious", "subject to maternal instinct"). Most synonyms are similar in denotation but differ in connotative, stylistic or affective meaning. For example, *anger* (which is a general term), *rage* (which indicates loss of self-control), *fury* (which indicates overmastering destructive rage verging on madness), *indignation* (which indicates righteous anger) and *wrath* (which indicates rage or indignation accompanied by a desire to avenge, e.g. "The Grapes of Wrath"). It is obvious that connotative meanings vary from individual to individual according to culture, historical period, and experience. Connotative meaning is indeterminate and open-ended in a sense in which conceptual meaning is not. And connotative meaning is not specific to language, but is shared by other communicative systems, such as visual art and music.

In philosophy, denotation involves the relationship between a linguistic unit and the non-linguistic entities to which it refers. Thus, it is equivalent to referential meaning. For example, the denotation of human is any person such as *John* and *Mary*. Opposite to denotation, connotation means the properties of the entity a word denotes. For example, the connotation of human is "biped", "featherless", "rational", etc.

Social meaning is that which a piece of language conveys about the social circumstances of its use. For example, we recognize some words or pronunciations as being dialectal, i.e. as telling us something of the geographical or social origin of the speaker; other features of language tell us something of the social relationship between the speaker and hearer: we have a scale of "status" usage, e.g. descending from formal and literary English at one end to colloquial, familiar and eventually slang English at the other. For example, *steed* (poetic), *horse* (general), *nag* (slang), and *gee-gee* (baby language) are a group of synonyms, each of which demonstrates a distinctive stylistic meaning shown in the brackets.

Affective meaning indicates the personal feelings of the speaker, including his attitude to the listener, or his attitude to something he is talking about. It is often explicitly conveyed through the conceptual or connotative content of the words used. Interjections are to express emotions. Besides, some words explicitly convey emotive meanings: *good, bad, love, hate, modest, honest, angel, gang, freedom, tyrant, patriotic, traitor*. These words are called snarl words or purr words. Snarl words are words whose conceptual meaning becomes irrelevant because whoever is using them is simply capitalizing on their unfavorable connotations in order to give forceful expression to his own hostility, showing the speaker's disapproval and pejoration. Purr words are those to express the speaker's approval and appreciation. The following pairs of words illustrate this contrast of affective meaning: *black/ nigger, resolute/ obstinate, shrewd/ crafty, childlike/ childish, stout/ fat, slender/skinny, stateman/ politician, famous/ notorious*. The first word in each pair is appreciatory while the second is derogatory.

Reflected meaning is the meaning which arises in cases of multiple conceptual meaning, when one sense of a word forms part of our response to another sense. In the case of reflected meaning, more than one meaning surfaces at the same time, so there is a kind of ambiguity. It is as if one or more unintended meanings were inevitably thrown back like light or sound reflected on a surface. Sometimes, such coincidental, "unwanted"meanings cause us to change a lexical item for another. For example, *dear* in the expression "my dear old car" may be misinterpreted as meaning "expensive", thus we can substitute "lovely" and eliminate the potential ambiguity. People generally choose to use euphemistic expressions or avoid using taboo words to keep away from the reflected meanings associated with some certain words. Taboo words concerned with sex or religion are seldom used simply because they usually conjure up uncomfortable associations.

Collocative meaning consists of the associations a word acquires on account of the meanings of words which tend to occur in its environment. For example, *pretty* and *handsome* share common ground in the meaning "good-looking", but may be distinguished by the range of nouns with which they are likely to collocate: *pretty* is usually used with girl, while *handsome* is usually used with boy. Further examples are quasi-synonymous verbs such as *wander* and *stroll* (*cows* may *wander*, but may not *stroll*), *tremble* and *quiver* (one *trembles* with *fear*, but *quivers* with *excitement*).

Thematic meaning is what is communicated by the way in which a speaker or writer organizes the message, in terms of ordering, focus, and emphasis. An active sentence has a different meaning from its passive equivalent, although in conceptual content they seem to be the same. The difference lies in the communicative values because the two sentences suggest different contexts. For example, the active sentence *The rain destroyed the crops.* seems to answer an implicit question *What did the rain do?*, while the passive sentence *The crops were destroyed by the rain.* seems to answer an implicit question *What happened to the crops?* Thematic meaning is mainly a matter of choice between alternative grammatical constructions such as passive voice, inversion, cleft sentence, and so on. Another pair of examples are: 1) *Nothing will turn us from this.* And 2) *From this nothing will turn us.* These two sentences start with different themes, which indicate different contexts.

5.4.3 Semantic Field

A semantic field is a set of words (or lexemes) related in meaning. Linguist Adrienne Lehrer has defined semantic field more specifically as "a set of lexemes which cover a certain conceptual domain and which bear certain specifiable relations to one another" (1985: 283–296). Semantic fields are defined by subject matter, such as body parts, landforms, diseases, colors, foods, or kinship relations. The words in a semantic field share a common semantic property. For example, the field of "kinship" includes terms such as *father, mother, brother, sister, uncle, aunt* and etc. Another example is the semantic field of "furniture", including terms such as *chair, bed, settee, stool, table* and etc.

In a semantic field, meanings of words are dependent and incompatible. For example, the field of "week" includes terms: *Sunday, Monday, Tuesday, ⋯ Saturday*. The terms present a sequence of the seven days of a week, and thus runs in a circle. "*It was on Saturday that she went there*" implies that she did not go there on Monday or any other day of the week.

In a semantic field, not all lexical items necessarily have the same status. Consider the following sets, which together form the semantic field of color terms: 1) *Blue, red, yellow, green, black, purple*; 2) *Indigo, saffron, royal blue, aquamarine, bisque*. The colors referred to by the words of Set 1 are more "usual" than those described in Set 2. They are said to be less marked members of the semantic field than those of Set 2. The less marked members of a semantic field are usually easier to learn and remember than more marked members. Children learn the term *blue* before they learn the terms *indigo, royal blue*, or *aquamarine*. Often, a less marked word consists of only one morpheme, in contrast to more marked words (contrast *blue* with *royal blue* or *aquamarine*). The less marked member of a semantic field cannot be described by using the name of another member of the same field, whereas more marked members can be thus described (*indigo* is a kind of *blue*, but *blue* is not a kind of *indigo*). Less marked terms also tend to be used more frequently than more marked terms; for example, *blue* occurs considerably more frequently in conversation and writing than *indigo* or *aquamarine*. Less marked terms are also often broader in meaning than more marked terms. Finally, less marked words are not the result of the metaphorical usage of the name of another object or concept, whereas more marked words often are (https://www.thoughtco.com/semantic-field-1692079) .

It is to be noted that there are cultural contexts behind semantic field, for example, the members of the semantic field of "kinship" are different between English and Chinese. *Uncle* is an inclusive term in English which is correspondent to the chinese terms 叔父，伯父，姑父，舅父，姨父；and *Aunt* is correspondent to the Chinese terms 婶婶，大娘，姑姑，姨母，舅母 .

5.4.4 Sense Relations

Words are in different sense relations with each other. Words can be categorized on the paradigmatic axis into synonyms, antonyms, hyponyms and meronyms according to the relationships between their senses, in terms of the semantic relations of similarity, contrast, inclusion and part-whole relation. Sense relations also include polysemy and homonymy. Polysemy has to do with how different meanings of the same word are related, while homonymy has to do with how different meanings are related to words of the same phonological and/ or spelling form.

5.4.4.1 Synonymy

Synonymy refers to sameness of meaning. A synonym is a word having the same or almost the same meaning as another word in the same language. In the development of English language, its vocabulary has mainly come from two sources: Anglo-Saxon on the one hand and French, Latin, and Greek on the other. As a result, English is rich in synonyms, with pairs of words from different origins expressing the same meaning. For example, *start/ commence, buy/ purchase, danger/ hazard, reduce/ decrease, fire/ conflagration, car/ automobile, time/ epoch* and many others.

With absolute synonyms, the meaning and function of the synonymous words are exactly the same. This condition is very rare. An example of an absolute synonym is *airport* and *aerodrome*. The former is what we commonly use nowadays, whereas the latter is an old-fashioned word. On the other hand, most synonyms in English are actually relative synonyms or near-synonyms. These synonyms can differ in their collocation, register, and regional/social variation.

Firstly, synonyms may convey different shades of meaning, and thus vary in the range and intensity of meaning. For example, *anger, rage, and wrath* are synonymous, but differ in terms of range and intensity. Of the three words, *anger* is the most general and has the widest range of meaning while *rage* implies "violent anger that is difficult to control", and *wrath* implies "strong vengeful anger". Secondly, synonyms may belong to different dialects of the language. An obvious example is the difference between American English and British English. For example, the pairs of *fall/ autumn, apartment/ flat, subway/ underground, sidewalk/pavement.* Thirdly, some synonyms convey difference of formality. For example, the sets of *kid/ child/ offspring, start/ begin/ commence, guy (boy)/ man/ gentleman*. Fourthly, synonyms may have the same conceptual meaning but different emotive or evaluative meanings. For example, the pairs of *collaborator/ accomplice, attract/ lure*. The former ones imply approval, while the latter ones imply disapproval. Fifthly, synonyms may collocate with different other words in their actual usage. For example, *accuse···of···, charge···with···, sue/ prosecute/ indict ··· for···*.

In text level, synonyms are frequently used as an efficient cohesive device. The use of synonyms is one of the five types of cohesion by Halliday and Hasan: As a cohesive device, lexical reiteration is the repetition of a lexical item, or the occurrence of a synonym of some kind, in the context of reference; that is, where two occurrences have the same referent (Halliday & Hasan, 2001: 318).

5.4.4.2 Antonymy

Antonymy refers to oppositeness of meaning. Words having opposite meanings are antonyms. Antonyms can be classified into three main sub-types: gradable antonyms, complementary antonyms, and converse antonyms.

Gradable antonyms are a pair of antonyms where the two words lie on a continuous spectrum, and there are often intermediate forms between the two members of the pair. Length is such a continuous spectrum so *long* and *short*, two words on opposite ends of the spectrum, are gradable antonyms. Other examples include: *heavy/ light, big/ small, young/ old, empty/ full, dull/ interesting*. There are three characteristics of gradable antonyms: 1) They are gradable. The members of a pair differ in terms of degree. The denial of one is not necessarily the assertion of the other. They can be modified by "very". 2) Antonyms of this kind are graded against different norms. The criterion varies with the object described. We can say *a big car*, while *a small plane*; *a microcomputer*, and *a microorganism*. 3) One member of a pair, usually the term for the higher degree, serves as the cover term 涵盖词 , e.g. *How old are you?* The cover term is "unmarked" (i.e. usual) and the covered "marked" or unusual, e.g. *how young are you?* The latter question will not be used unless we deliberately emphasize the point that the addressee is surprisingly or unexpectedly young.

Complementary antonyms are a pair of antonyms where the two words do not lie on a continuous spectrum, and the denial of one member of the pair implies the assertion of the other. There is no continuous spectrum between *male* and *female* and the denial of *male* implies the assertion of *female*, and therefore they are complementary antonyms. Other examples include: *odd/ even, exit/ entrance, alive/ dead, pass/ fail, boy/ girl, present/ absent, and innocent/ guilty*.

Converse or relational opposites exhibit the reversal of the relationship between the two items, one presupposes the other. There is no lexical opposite of *teacher*, but *teacher* and *student* are opposite within the context of their relationship. This makes them relational antonyms. Other examples include: *husband/ wife, doctor/ patient, parent/ child, employer/ employee, buy/ sell, above/ below, give/ receive,* and *borrow/ lend.*

Besides the above three main types of antonyms, Leech mentions other less common types of semantic opposition such as hierarchic opposition, e.g. *inch/ foot/ yard*, and cyclic hierarchic opposition such as "days of the week" (Leech, 1981: 106–107).

Antonymy can be used in figures of speech. Oxymoron and antithesis are based on antonymy. The use of gradable antonyms may give rise to fuzziness.

5.4.4.3 Hyponymy

Hyponymy is meaning inclusiveness or a matter of class membership. It shows the relationship between B (a generic term) and A (A is a specific instance of B). A is included or a kind of B, e.g. chair and furniture, rose and flower. The more general term of the pair is called superordinate/ hypernym; and the more specific term is called hyponym. A superordinate term can have many hyponyms. Hyponyms having the same superordinate are called co-hyponyms.

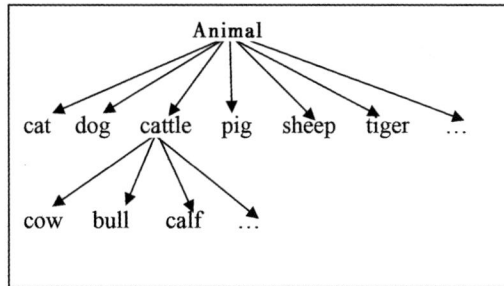

If X is superordinate of Y, and Y in turn is the superordinate of Z, then X is also the superordinate of Z as illustrated in the above chart. From this example, we can see one term may be a hyponym in one hierarchical relation but a superordinate in another.

5.4.4.4 Meronymy

Meronymy, which originates from Greek (*mero* means "part", *onuma* means "name"), is a part-whole relation that lexical items may have. In this relation, the part is called a meronym, and the whole is called a holonym. For example, *engine* is a meronym of *car* which is its holonym.

Meronymy demonstrates the idea of "is part of", while hyponymy demonstrates the idea of "is a kind of". For example, an *oak tree* is a kind of *tree*, but a *leaf* is part of a *tree*.

5.4.4.5 Polysemy

Polysemy refers to the phenomenon that the same one word may have multiple related meanings. For example, *table* is a polysemic word, as it has several different meanings: 1) a piece of furniture; 2) the people sitting at a table for a meal; 3) a list of facts or numbers arranged in a special order; and etc.

There are two main ways in which meanings of a polysemic word are usually related: radiation and concatenation. Semantically, radiation is the process in which the primary or central meaning stands at the center while secondary meanings radiate from it in every direction like rays. For example, the word *head* originally means "part of the body on top of the neck", and a number of derived meanings radiate from this basic meaning, such as "the mind or brain", "the person in charge of an organization", "the top part of something", "used to say how many animals of a particular type are on a farm", etc. Concatenation is a semantic process in which the meaning of a word moves gradually away from its first sense by successive shifts, like the links of a chain, until there is no connection between the sense that is finally developed and the primary meaning. For example, the word *board* originally means "a flat piece of wood", and there are a number of derivative meanings such as "a piece of wood for a special purpose", "a table especially one set for serving food", "the tablet on which games are played", "any piece of furniture resembling a table", and "a group of people who have power to make decisions and control a company".

A polysemic word is the result of the evolution of the primary meaning of the word (of the same etymology); while complete homonyms are of different etymologies, and they look alike by coincidence. Also, meanings of a polysemic word are of relevant relation and the meanings are listed under one item in the dictionary; while homonyms are different items in the dictionary.

5.4.4.6 Homonymy

Homonymy is the semantic relationship between words that are homonyms—words that have different meanings but are pronounced the same or spelled the same or both. There are three types of homonyms in English: homophones, homographs and complete homonyms.

Words that are identical in pronunciation, but differ in spelling and meanings are called homophones, e.g. *night/ knight, rain/ reign, sea/ see, air/ heir.*

Words that have the same spelling, but differ in pronunciation and meaning are called homographs, e.g. *tear(n.)/ tear(v.), lead(n.)/ lead(v.), wind (n.)/ wind (v.).*

Words that are identical in pronunciation and spelling but different in meaning are called complete homonyms, e.g. 1) A river is the richest thing in the world, because it has two *banks*. 2) If we don't *hang* together, we'll *hang* separately. 3) A professor tapped on his desk and shouted: "Gentlemen—*order*!" The entire class yelled, "Beer!".

From the sentence examples above, we find pun—a figure of speech which is a humorous use of homonyms.

5.4.5 Word of Chinese

5.4.5.1 汉语同义词文化：骈词中的同义连用现象

在汉语词汇的构词发展过程中，既有新旧交替，也有古今结合——骈词（doublets）。骈词是一个词的旧形式和新形式同时存在，旧形式往往只残存在书面语言里，而新形式则在口语里（王，2015：48）。骈词这种构词法与语音和语义都有联系。

骈词可以合成双音词。例如上古音的"呼"[xua]，变为中古音的"唤"[xuan]，"呼"和"唤"就是骈词。骈词大约可以分为两类：第一类是声母和主要元音都相同，只是鼻音韵尾或有或无，这叫作"对转"或"阴阳对转"，如"呼唤、饴糖"。第二类是主要元音相近，叫作"旁转"（王，2015：48)。有时候连主要元音也完全相同，只是韵头小异或声母小异，如"域国"、"观看"[kuan k'an]。古代汉语的构词法是不断发展的。上古汉语是以单音词为主的。从先秦的史料看来，汉语已经不是纯粹的单音节语。就名词来说，"国家、天下、君子、大夫"等，已经老早由短语变了单词。形容词、动词也有了双音词。到了中古时期，双音词逐渐增加。汉语由单音词过渡到双音词的发展，是汉语发展的内部规律之一（王，2015：333–337）。汉语词汇由单音词向复音词发展，增强了语言表达的精确性（尤其是对于汉语这种声调语言）。

语义方面，骈词同出一词，同义连用是古代汉语中一种普遍存在的骈词构词法。同义连用是指两个或两个以上意义相同、相近或相类的词并连在一起使用，在句中表示一个相对完整的意义，充当一个语法成分的语言现象。它有着语素凝固的不稳定性、结构组合的灵活性、词序的不固定性和意义的完整性等特点。由于有些同义词经常连用在一起，后来就发展成为一个复音词。汉语大部分的双音词都是经过同义词临时组合的阶段的，由短语发展成为复合词，再发展成为复音词（王，2015：337）。

朋友

父子有亲，君臣有义，夫妇有别，长幼有序，朋友有信。《孟子·滕文公上》

翘翘车乘，招我以弓。岂不欲往，畏我友朋。《左传·庄公二十二年》

朋：朋友，古代特指受业同一师门的人。友：朋友，古代特指志同道合的人。郑玄注："同师为朋，同志为友。"词序颠倒前后都是朋友的意思，词性为名词。

社稷

"社"指土神及其受祭之所，如《说文·示部》："社，地主也。从示、土。"《礼记·效特性》："天子大社，必受霜露风雨，以达天地之气也。是故丧国之社屋之，不受天阳也。"

"稷"指谷神及其受祭之所，如《说文·禾部》："稷，穧也。五谷之长。从禾，畟声。"《汉书·郊祀志下》："圣汉兴，礼仪稍定，已有官社，未立官稷。遂于官社后立官稷，以夏禹配食官社，后稷配食官稷。稷种榖树。"但"社"和"稷"不是分别设坛的，而是合二为一的，统称"社稷"，如今北京社稷坛。

"社稷"一词可以指土神和谷神，《书·太甲上》："先王顾諟天之明命，以承上下神祇，社稷宗庙罔不祗肃。"但是在古籍中更多的用法是指国家。《礼记·檀弓下》："能执干戈以卫社稷，虽欲勿殇，不亦可乎？"《史记·秦始皇本纪》："是以君子为国，观之上古，验之当世，参以人事，察盛衰之理，审权势之宜，去就有序，变化有时，故旷日长久而社稷安矣。"《汉书·文帝纪》："丞相平等皆曰：'臣伏计之，大王奉高祖宗庙最宜称，虽天下诸侯万民，皆以为宜。臣等为宗庙社稷计，不敢忽。'""社稷"指国家时，与原来的词义有一定的关系，但不是完全对应，有一定的差别。

恭敬

恭敬之心，人皆有之。《孟子·告子上》

敬恭明神，宜无悔怒。《诗·大雅》

恭：《说文·心部》："恭，肃也。"恭敬，有礼貌。《礼记·曲礼上》："在貌为恭，在心为敬，是以君子恭敬蹲节。"敬：《说文·苟部》："敬，肃也。"恭敬，严肃，认真。"恭敬"为同义连用与颠倒后形成"敬恭"，都表示"恭敬、有礼貌"的意思。"恭"和"敬"都是形容词，连用后所形成的"恭敬""敬恭"也是形容词。

器械

百工有器械之巧则壮。《庄子·徐无鬼》

以粟易械器者，不为厉陶冶；陶冶亦以其械器易粟者，岂为厉农夫哉？《孟子·滕文公上》

器：用具、器具。械：枷粗、镣铐之类的刑具，泛指器械，器具。词序颠倒前后都表示器械器具，而且都是名词。

谨慎

主信爱之，则谨慎而嗛。《荀子·仲尼》

然后恭敬以先之，忠信以统之，慎谨以行之，端息以守之。《荀子·仲尼》

谨：谨慎，慎重。慎：谨慎，慎重。词序颠倒前后都是"言行慎重小心，以免发生有害或不幸的事情"的意思，而且都用作形容词（刘，2010）。

5.4.5.2 汉语反义词文化

汉语反义词分为以下几种：第一，两个反义词的意义处在两个极限，具有极性的对立关系，如"大/小、厚/薄、新/故、长/短"等，它们之间存在着中间状态。第二，两个反义词的意义之间具有互补关系，否定此一方即意味着肯定另一方，它们之间不存在中间状态，如"男/女、彼/此、有/无、生/死"等。第三，两个反义词所表示的事物只是在某种关系上构成的对立：由时空关系构成对立的词有"春/秋、古/今、南/北、上/下、天/地、日/月"等；由社会关系构成对立的词有"君/臣、父/子、夫/妻"等；由修辞关系构成对立的词有"尧/跖、嫫母/西施、燕雀/鸿鹄"等。第四，两个反义词所表示的反向动作构成了意义上的对立，如"出/入、俯/仰、进/退、去/从、呼/吸"等（赵，1986）。无论是在古文还是在现代汉语中，反义词的运用可以使语言表达更加鲜明，结构对称，增加修辞效果。与英语反义词分类相比，由修辞关系构成对立的词更加反映汉语语言文化特色。

　　陈胜者，阳城人也，字涉。吴广者，阳夏人也，字叔。陈涉少时，尝与人佣耕，辍耕之垄上，怅恨久之，曰："苟富贵，无相忘。"佣者笑而应曰："若为佣耕，何富贵也？"陈涉叹息曰："嗟乎，燕雀安知鸿鹄之志哉！"《史记·陈涉世家》

　　子曰："温故而知新，可以为师矣。"《论语》

　　昔我往矣，杨柳依依；今我来思，雨雪霏霏。《小雅·采薇》

知否，知否，应是绿肥红瘦。李清照《如梦令》

要完全地反映整个的事物，反映事物的本质，反映事物的内部规律性，就必须经过思考作用，将丰富的感觉材料加以去粗取精、去伪存真、由此及彼、由表及里的改造制作工夫，造成概念和理论的系统，就必须从感性认识跃进到理性认识。毛泽东《实践论》

5.5 Sentence Meaning

5.5.1 Definition of Sentence Meaning

Bloomfield defines sentences as the maximum free units of language. Sentences play an important role in our daily verbal communication. According to Saeed (2009: 11), sentence meaning is compositional. Sentence meaning is determined by the meaning of its component parts and the way in which they are combined. For example, sentence "John gave Mary a bunch of flowers." and sentence "Mary gave John a bunch of flowers." differ in meaning. The former sentence takes "John" as actor of the verb "gave", "a bunch of flowers" as its direct object and "Mary" as the receptor. While the latter sentence takes "Mary" as actor of the verb "gave, "and "John" as the receptor. Thus, the meaning of the latter sentence is opposite to the former one.

With his lexicon and grammar, a native speaker can understand sentence meaning naturally in daily communication. The same will be true of mastering a second language.

5.5.2 Contrast of Chinese and English

汉英句法存在差异。汉语句法重意合，如"吃食堂 / 吃饭、晒太阳 / 晒被子、看病 / 看医生"。而英语句法以形显义，句中的词语或分句之间用语言形式手段（如关联词）连接起来，表达语法意义和逻辑关系（连，1993: 48）。这在汉英句法结构对比中是基本差异，Leech (1981: 183–196) 从语义学的角度有新的总结。

Dummy verb *be* in English SVC sentence pattern: in English sentence pattern SVC (e.g. *Fred is very ill.*), it just happens that English sentences require a verb phrase, and where no content capable of being expressed by a verb is present, the "dummy verb" *be* has to be introduced to fill out the structure of the sentence.

The above verb *be* can be regarded as a "dummy element" in syntax, that is, as an element which exists on the syntactic level to fulfill certain conditions of syntactic well–formedness, but which has no semantic content. Another example of **a dummy element is the subject *it***in sentences like *It is raining.* "Rain" is a semantic predicate which is without arguments; however, syntax requires that a sentence should have a subject, and so the pronoun *it* is introduced to fill this grammatical function, even though it has no conceptual content to express.

Other examples of dummy elements:

1) X: **There** was a bracelet in the box.

   Y: A bracelet was in the box.

2) X: **It** surprises me that he has left.

   Y: That he has left surprises me.

The above examples demonstrate dummy element *there* in English "there be…" sentence type, and the dummy subject *it* in the English syntactic rule which postpones a clausal subject to the end of the sentence.

5.5.3 Sense Relations between Sentences

The same as sense relations between words, there exist sense relations between sentences. The main types of sense relations between sentences are synonymy, inconsistency, entailment, presupposition and implicature.

5.5.3.1 Synonymy

Sentences may be synonymous or form paraphrases. A paraphrase is an alternative version of a sentence that conveys the same meaning with the original sentence. Synonymous sentences or paraphrases have the same truth value in logic. For example:

1) X: He was a bachelor all his life.

    Y: He never got married all his life.

2) X: The boy killed the cat.

    Y: The cat was killed by the boy.

Sentences X and Y mean approximately the same, differing only in ways of expression. The synonymous sentences or paraphrases may be expressed in logic as follows: If X is true, Y is true; if X is false, Y is false; and vice versa.

5.5.3.2 Inconsistency

Inconsistency or contradiction means that if one sentence is true, the other must be false. For example:

    1) X: He is single.

       Y: He has a wife.

    2) X: This is my first visit to Beijing.

       Y: I have been to Beijing twice.

Sentences X and Y are inconsistent or contradictory to each other, which means one sentence does not follow logically from the other. That is, if X is true, Y is false; if X is false, Y is true.

5.5.3.3 Entailment

Entailment is a relation of inclusion. If X entails Y, then the meaning of Y is included in X. For example:

    1) X: John married a blond heiress.

       Y: John married a blond.

    2) X: Mary has been to Beijing.

       Y: Mary has been to China.

In the above examples, sentences X contain words which have all the semantic components of a word used in sentences Y. In logic, If X is true, Y is necessarily true; if X is false, Y may be true or false.

5.5.3.4 Presupposition

Presupposition is a statement tacitly assumed beforehand at the beginning of another statement. For example, in the following pairs of sentences, sentences X presuppose sentences Y.

    1) X: His bike needs repairing.

       Y: He has a bike.

    2) X: Paul has given up smoking.

       Y: Paul once smoked.

In the above examples, Y is a condition that must be met in order for the intended meaning of a sentence to be regarded as acceptable. That is to say, if sentences Y are not true, sentences X would not be acceptable in the real world. In 1), if he does not have a bike, there would be no statement like *"His bike needs repairing"*. In logic, If X is true, Y must be true; If X is false, Y is still true. In other words, both X and its negation presuppose Y, which is different from entailment.

5.5.3.5 Implicature

Implicature is largely a relation of pragmatic implication, which is worked out on the basis of the literal meaning of the sentence and the context. For example,

    1) Peter: Would you drive a Mercedes?

       Mary: I would not drive any expensive car.

    Implicature: Mary would not drive a Mercedes.

    implicature is the implied meaning inferred from a sentence in terms of the speaker's and the hearer's assumptions and beliefs.

5.6 Semantic Analysis

5.6.1 Componential Analysis

In semantic analysis of word meaning, componential analysis (CA) is to analyze word meaning into a set of semantic features. The word *man*, for example, has the following semantic features: [Human], [Adult], [Male].

Semantic features constitute the linguistic meaning of a word. They are a set of abstracted characteristics that distinguish the category of the word from all other categories. Semantic features are established on the basis of binary oppositions. For example, the semantic feature [± Male] can distinguish the following noun pairs:

man	woman
boy	girl
rooster	hen
bull	cow

And we can set up the semantic features [± Human], [± Adult] through the following two sets of words.

man	rooster
woman	hen
boy	bull
girl	cow

man	boy
woman	girl

Thus, we can set up three binary semantic features: [± Human], [± Adult], [± Male]. In making componential analysis of a word meaning, we can use "plus" or "minus" of the semantic features to specify the presence or absence of the semantic properties that define the word. For example:

man [+Male, +Adult, +Human]

woman [−Male, +Adult, +Human]

boy [+Male, −Adult, +Human]

girl [−Male, −Adult, +Human]

In the paper *The Structure of a Semantic Theory*, Katz and Fodor (1963) proposes the notion of Componential Analysis (CA): we require entries in a form exemplified in the following figure. Here the unenclosed elements are GRAMMATICAL MARKERS, the elements enclosed in parentheses are what we shall call SEMANTIC MARKERS, and the expressions enclosed in brackets are what we shall call DISTINGUISHERS. We have already commented upon the function of grammatical markers. The semantic markers and distinguishers are the means by which we can decompose the meaning of one sense of a lexical item into its atomic concepts, and thus exhibit the semantic structure in a dictionary entry and the semantic relations between dictionary entries. That is, the semantic relations among the various senses of a lexical item and among the various senses of different lexical items are represented by formal relations between markers and distinguishers.

Componential analysis can be used to explain sense relations clearly, such as synonymy, hyponymy, entailment, inconsistency, tautology and semantic anomaly. For example, because *Beijing* can be analyzed as [+Capital] [+China], including the meaning of *China*, so sentence *Mary has been to Beijing.* entails sentence *Mary has been to China.*

```
                        Bachelor
                           |
                         Noun
               (Human)                    (Animal)
        (Male)         [who has the       (Male)
     [who has          first or
      never     [young lowest         [young fur seal
     married]    knight academic      when without a
                 serving degree]      mate during the
                 under the            breeding time]
                 standard of
                 another knight]
```

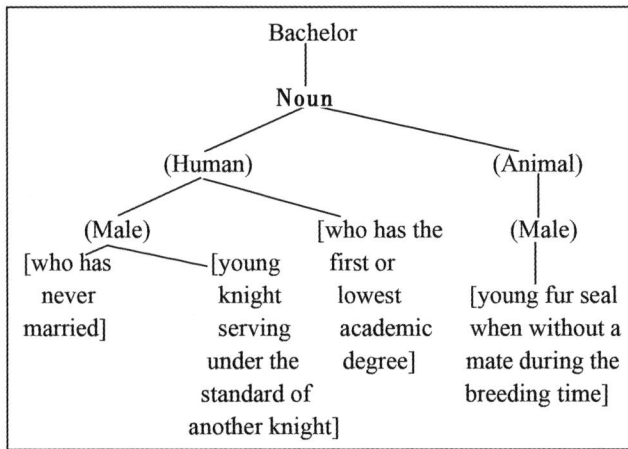

(Katz &Fodor, 1963:186)

At the same time, because semantic features is an artificial language itself, there still lacks a universal system of semantic features that can make an analysis of all lexical items in a language.

5.6.2 Predication Analysis

We can understand the numerous sentences in our daily verbal communication. But in philosophy and logic, we need to distinguish propositions from sentences. A sentence is a grammatical unit, while a proposition is a semantic unit. Lyons (1977) defines proposition as what is expressed by a declarative sentence when that sentence is uttered to make a statement. A proposition is the unit of meaning that identifies the subject matter of a statement. It describes some state of affairs, and takes the form of a declarative sentence. A proposition has a truth value. It is either true or false. Sentences having the same underlying proposition have the same truth value, because they share a description of the same state of affairs. For example:

    1) Julius Caesar conquered Britain.

    2) Britain was conquered by Julius Caesar.

    3) It was Britain that Julius Caesar conquered.

    4) It was Julius Caesar that conquered Britain.

All the sentences have the same proposition that can be expressed as Conquer (Caesar, Britain).

Propositions are efficient in presenting the meaning of a sentence especially in philosophy and logic. A proposition can be represented in various forms of sentences.

Another way to describe a sentence meaning is predication analysis proposed by Leech (1981: 124–131). For describing the meaning of sentences, as of words, a hierarchy of units is required. The major unit is predication, a common category shared by propositions, questions, commands, etc. For example, sentence *My uncle owns this car.* can be broken down into two arguments (or logical participants), *"my uncle"* and *"this car"*, with a relational element linking them ("owns"). This linking element may be called, following logical rather than grammatical terminology, a PREDICATE. Argument and predicate are constituents of the predications expressed by sentences.

Predicate and argument have different roles in the whole predication. The predicate is the major or pivotal element, and may be said to GOVERN the arguments, which are in a relation of dependency to it. The predicate is the major element in the sense that it determines the number and nature of the arguments. There is two-place predicate, which governs two arguments, e.g. *I love my family.* And there is one-place predicate which governs one argument, e.g. *John left.* And the predications are called two-place predications and one-place predications respectively.

This kind of analysis of breaking down predications into their constituents is called predication analysis. The predicate is the place where logical elements belonging to the complete predication as a whole are to be found: for example, tense, modality, and adverbial meanings. The predicate is also the main element of a predication in the sense that it cannot be dispensed with. Arguments can be omitted, and are variable in number. There are two-place predicate, one-place-predicate, and even no-place predicate, such as *It is raining.* or *It will be warm tomorrow.* Predication analysis is efficient in analyzing sense relations between sentences.

Further Readings:

Leech, G. 1981. *Semantics: The Study of Meaning, 2nd ed.* Harmondsworth: Penguin.

Lyons, J. 1995/2000. *Linguistic Semantics: An Introduction.* 北京：外语教学与研究出版社.

Ogden, C.K. & Richards, I.A. 1923. *The Meaning of Meaning.* London: Routledge & Kegan Paul.

Saeed, J. I. 2009. *Semantics 3rd ed.* 北京：外语教学与研究出版社.

徐炯列, 1995 /1990.《语义学》第二版, 北京：语文出版社.

Questions and Exercises:

1. Define the following terms:

   the sema ntic triangle, conceptual meaning, Leech's seven types of meaning, reference, sense, synonymy, antonymy, hyponymy, meronymy, polysemy, homonymy, semantic field, entailment, presupposition, componential analysis, predication analysis, proposition

2. What is sense? What is reference? How are they related?

3. Illustrate the difference between denotation and connotation with examples.

4. How are antonyms classified?

5. How are synonyms differentiated?

6. How are the meanings of a polysemic word related?

7. Look up the dictionary to find the meaning of "门" in Chinese. Tell the differences between polysemy and homonymy.

8. Summarize the corresponding figures of speech in which we make use of sense relations of words.

9. Find antonymy in figures of speech, and make a contrast between Chinese and English.

10. The meaning of a sentence is determined by the meaning of its component parts and the way in which they are combined. Comment on this statement with examples.

Chapter 6

───────

Pragmatics: The Use of Language in Context

语 言 学 导 论
新文科思政教程

6.1 Introduction

There are two branches of linguistics that study meaning. One is semantics, the other is pragmatics. Semantics studies the meaning of words and sentences. While pragmatics is the study of language use in context. For example,

1) It is cold here.

2) Wife: What's in the newspaper?

Husband: (putting down the newspaper and switching on the TV) Nothing.

Sentence 1) is a declaration, telling the hearer that the temperature is low literally. In everyday communication, there is more about the speaker's intention in making such an utterance. It may be a reminder made by a patient implying he has a fever; it may be uttered for requiring warming up the room, and it may convey other intentions of the speaker in specific contexts. In Sentence 2), the husband means more than the literal meaning of "Nothing", because any newspaper is not blank, and there must be news in it. The husband's utterance of "Nothing" means that "there is nothing worth reading in the newspaper." Pragmatics studies meaning beyond literal expressions in specific context. It is context that distinguishes pragmatics from semantics.

Learning Objectives:

1.Remember the following terms: constatives, performatives, locutionary act, illocutionary act, perlocutionary act, Searle's five types of illocutionary speech acts, Cooperative Principle, conversational implicature, Politeness Principle

2.Understand: The distinction between pragmatics and semantics

The notion of context

The Speech Act Theory

The Cooperative Principle and Politeness Principle

The difference between entailment and presupposition

3.Illustrate with examples: The Speech Act Theory

CP and violation of its maxims

Politeness Principle

4.To tell Chinese stories to illustrate politeness

Lead-in Questions:

1.Discussion on "pragmatic awareness" in native language and second language (English), e.g. 爷爷下班回家, 看见三岁的小孙子, 说: "XX, 你今天是不是还没有叫我呀？" 小孙子: "爷爷"。

2.Discussion on difference of "politeness" between Chinese and English, e.g. how to offer help to a senior citizen? How to get the name of a stranger?

6.2 Context

6.2.1 The Notion of Context

The notion of context is essential to the pragmatic study of language. It is generally considered as constituted by the knowledge shared by the speaker and hearer. Various components of shared knowledge have been identified, e.g. knowledge of the language they use, knowledge of what has been said before, knowledge about the world in general, knowledge about the specific situation in which linguistic communication is taking place, and knowledge about each other (Dai, 2002: 86).

6.2.2 Foreign Studies of Context

The notion of context of situation was coined by Bronislaw Malinowski (1923) in his paper *The Problem of Meaning in Primitive Languages* in Ogden and Richards' book *The Meaning of Meaning* (Ogden &Richards, 1923: 296–336). Through studying the culture of people living in a group of islands in the South Pacific Ocean, Malinowski made interesting observations about their language and the relationship between the language and the situation in which these people lived. He understood that a text written by these people could not be understood by any foreigners or by people living outside this community even if translated into their own languages because each message brought more meanings than those expressed through the words, meanings that could only be understood if accompanied by the situation. For example, "We paddle in place".

Malinowski emphasized the cultural context of situation in which an utterance was located. "Thus, starting from the wider idea of context, namely the study of any language, spoken by a people who live under conditions different from our own and possess a different culture, must be carried out in conjunction with the study of their culture and of their environment" (Malinowski, 1923: 306).

The theory of context of situation had been adopted by Systemic-Functional Linguistics and had been further developed. Malinowski's theory was indeed limited to some particular kind of texts, while there was the necessity of a model that could be applied to different kinds of texts and situations. British linguist John Rupert Firth argued that language represents a set of events which speakers uttered—an action one learned in doing things. He believed that whatever one said must be understood in the context of situation. Thus, besides linguistic factors, factors like the social status and personal history of the speaker, as well as the social character of the situation, must also be taken into account. It was Firth who in 1950 proposed a development of Malinowski's idea, which consisted in a framework of features that should be used as referential points to characterize the context of situation of a text. This framework was made up of four headings:

A. the Participants in the situation

B. the Action of the participants

C. other Relevant Features of the situation

D. the Effects of the verbal action

After that, M.A.K. Halliday proposed the concept of "register" in the 1960s and 1970s, which "can be defined as a configuration of meanings that are typically associated with a particular situational configuration of field, mode, and tenor." (Halliday, 1990: 38). The linguistic features (specific expressions, lexico–grammatical and phonological features) and the particular values of the three dimensions of field, mode and tenor determine the functional variety of a language (Halliday, 1994: 22). These three parameters can be used to specify the context of situation in which language is used. Field of discourse is defined as "the total event, in which the text is functioning, together with the purposive activity of the speaker or writer; it thus includes the subject–matter as one element in it" (Halliday, 1994: 22). The field describes activities and processes that are happening at the time of speech. The analysis of this parameter focuses on the entire situation, e.g. when a mother talks to her child. The mode of discourse refers to "the function of the text in the event, including therefore both the channel taken by the language–spoken or written, extempore or prepared–and its genre, or rhetorical mode, as narrative, didactic, persuasive, 'phatic communion' and so on" (Halliday, 1994: 22). This variable determines the role and function of language in a particular situation. When analyzing the mode of a text, the main question is "What is achieved by the use of language in this context?" For example, a fairy tale (in written form) may have a narrative or entertaining function. A spoken conversation can be argumentative (in a discussion) or phatic. Tenor of discourse describes the people that take part in an event as well as their relationships and statuses. "The tenor refers to the type of role interaction, the set of relevant social relations, permanent and temporary, among the participants involved" (Halliday, 1994: 22). There might be a specific hierarchy between the interlocutors, e.g. when the head of a business talks to an employee; or they may have only a temporary relationship, e.g. when a person asks an unknown pedestrian for the time.

6.2.3 Studies of Context in China

语境和语境的重要作用，早在我国的传统语文学就已经注意到了。例如，唐孔颖达《正义》说："褒贬虽在一字，不可单书一字以见褒贬，……经之字也，一字异不得成为一义，故经必须数句以成言。"这就是说，春秋笔法虽一字见褒贬，但必须有数句作为上下文，褒贬才能准确地显示出来，即"数句"是"一字"的语境。南朝刘勰《文心雕龙·章句》中说："人之立言，因字而生句，积句而成章，积章而成篇。篇之彪悍，章无疵也；章之明靡，句无玷也；句之精英，字无妄也。"这表明，刘勰已经从字、句、章、篇的相互关系来说明上下文（语境）对话语意义的表达和理解的重要作用了。

到 20 世纪 30 年代，我国语言学界对语境和语境的重要作用（主要是从修辞学角度）更有了一些重要的新认识。陈望道在 1932 年出版的《修辞学发凡》中说："修辞学以适应题旨情境为第一义，不应是仅仅语辞的修饰，更不应是离开情意的修饰。……凡成功的修辞，必定能够适合内容复杂的题旨，内容复杂的情境。极尽语言文字的可能性，使人觉得无可移易，至少写说者自己以为无可移易。"在此，陈望道提出了"题旨"与"情境"相适应的理论：认为只有做到使"内容复杂的题旨"与"内容复杂的情境"相适合，才能称之为"成功的修饰"。陈望道提出的"情境"显然就是弗思提出的"情景语境"。在《修辞学发凡》中，陈望道还提出了"六何"，即"何故"、"何事"、"何人"、"何地"、"何使"、"何如"（1979：7-8）。很明显，陈望道提出的"六何"就是构成语境的基本要素。他不仅提出了构成语境的要素，而且还阐明了修辞对语境的依赖关系，即"我们知道切实的自然的积极修辞多半是对应情境的"（1979：10）。

索振羽（2000, 23）认为，语境是人们运用自然语言进行言语交际的言语环境。语境包括上下文语境、情景语境（包括时间、地点、话题、场合和交际参与者）和民族文化传统语境（包括历史文化背景、社会规范和习俗、价值观）。

例如：

A．情景语境——话题

赵老："测量队到了，给咱看地势，好修沟！"

四嫂："修沟？修咱们的龙须沟！"

赵老："就是！修这条从来没人管的臭沟！"

四嫂："赵大爷，我，我磕个响头！"（跪下，磕了个头）

二春："这太棒了！想想看，没了臭水，没了臭味，没了苍蝇，没了蚊子，呕，太棒了！赵大爷，恶霸没了，又这么一修沟，咱们这儿不快变成东安市场？从此，谁敢再说政府半句坏话，我就掰下他的脑袋来！"——老舍《龙须沟》

这段对话表达的话题是龙须沟居民赞颂人民政府爱民修沟（索，2000: 25）。

B．民族文化传统语境——历史典故、生活习俗

黛玉听见宝玉奚落宝钗，心中着实得意，才要搭言，也趁势取个笑儿，不想靛儿因找扇子，宝钗又发了两句话，他便改口说道："宝姐姐，你听了两出什么戏？"宝钗因见黛玉面上有得意之态，一定是听了宝玉方才奚落之言，遂了他的心愿，忽又见他问这话，便笑道："我看的是李逵骂了宋江，后来又赔不是。"宝玉便笑道："姐姐通今博古，色色都知道，怎么连这一出戏的名儿也不知道，就说了这么一套？这叫做《负荆请罪》。"宝钗笑道："原来这叫《负荆请罪》！你们通今博古，才知道'负荆请罪'；我不知什么叫'负荆请罪'！"

一句话未说了，宝玉黛玉二人心里有病，听了这话，早把脸羞红了。凤姐这些上虽不通，但只看他三人的形景，便知其意，也笑问道："这么大热的天，谁还吃生姜呢？"众人不解，便道："没有吃生姜的。"凤姐故意用手摸着腮，诧异道："既没人吃生姜，怎么这么辣辣的呢？"宝玉黛玉二人听见这话，越发不好意思了。宝钗再欲说话，见宝玉十分羞愧，形景改变，也就不好再说，只得一笑收住。别人总没解过他们四个人的话来，因此，付之一笑。——曹雪芹《红楼梦》第三十回

上面所选对话中，"负荆请罪"是中国历史典故，"姜"是中国人的日常食材。在对话或阅读中，如果缺少具体涉及的文化语境知识，势必造成对对话内容理解的失真。

6.3 Pragmatics, Syntax and Semantics

Pragmatics as a branch of study has its origin in semiotics. The term "pragmatics" was first proposed by Morris (1938) in his book *Foundations of the Theory of Signs*. Morris categorized pragmatics as one of the three components of semiotics, the other two being syntax and semantics:

Syntax is the study of the relationships between linguistics forms, how they are arranged in sequence and which sequences are well-formed.

Semantics is the study of the relationships between linguistic forms and entities in the world, how words literally connect to things.

Pragmatics is the study of the relation of linguistic units to their users.

Semantics studies literal, structural or lexical meaning, while pragmatics studies non-literal, implicit, intended meaning, or speaker meaning. Semantics is context independent, decontextualized, while pragmatics is context dependent, contextualized. Semantics deals with what is said, while pragmatics deals with what is implicated or inferred. Sentence meaning is determined by the meaning of its component parts and the way in which they are combined. It is the abstract context-independent entity called semantic proposition. While utterance meaning is context-dependent. It is the product of sentence meaning and context. Therefore, it is richer than sentence meaning.

Pragmatics also differs from syntax in that pragmatics is concerned with the appropriateness of naturally occurring utterances. For example, the four utterances in the following dialogue are all syntactically incomplete, but pragmatically they are all "appropriate" in the particular context.

Jane: Coffee?

Steve: Sure.

Jane: White?

Steve: White.

Morris sees pragmatics as the study of "all the psychological, biological, and sociological phenomena which occur in the functioning of signs" (Morris, 1938: 108). Yule defines pragmatics as "the study of speaker meaning, the study of contextual meaning, the study of how more gets communicated than is said, and the study of the expression of relative distance" (Yule, 1996: 1). In modern linguistics, pragmatics has come to be applied to the study of language from the viewpoint of the users, especially the choices they make, the constraints they encounter in using language in social interaction, and the effects their use of language has on other participants in an act of communication (Crystal, 1985: 240). Thus, pragmatics is function−oriented. It overlaps with principles of sociology and psychology. This chapter will introduce classic pragmatic theories which summarize these social and psychological rules we encounter in our use of language in specific contexts.

6.4 Speech Act Theory

The first major theory of pragmatics is Speech Act Theory initiated by Oxford Philosopher John Langshaw Austin in the late 1950s. In 1955, when he went to America to deliver William James lectures, he revised the notes and changed the title from *Words and Deeds* to *How to Do Things with Words*, which was published posthumously in 1962. Speech Act Theory was further developed by his American pupil John Searle in the 1960s and 1970s. A speech act can be regarded as a unit of utterance in communication that performs a certain function, i.e. an act of doing things with words.

6.4.1 Constatives and Performatives

It was for too long the assumption of philosophers that the business of a "statement" can only be to "describe" some state of affairs, or to "state some fact", which it must do either truly or falsely. Austin classified these statements as constatives. Constatives do not change the state of affairs. And a performative utterance (a performative) as the issuing of the utterance is the performing of an action. For performatives: A. they do not "describe" or "report" or constate anything at all, are not "true or false"; and B. the uttering of the sentence is, or is a part of, the doing of an action, which again would not normally be described as saying something (Austin, 1962: 2–5). Performatives bring about some immediate change to the state of affairs. For example:

1) China is one of the four ancient civilizations.

2) The earth revolves around the sun.

3) Water boils at 100℃ .

4) The judge sentenced the man to eight years in prison because he had robbed a bank.

5) "I do (take this lady to be my lawful wedded wife)" – as uttered in the course of the marriage ceremony.

6) "I name this ship Victoria" – as uttered when smashing the bottle against the stem.

7) "I give and bequeath my watch to my son" – as occurring in a will.

8) "I bet you sixpence it will rain tomorrow."

Clearly, Sentence 1) makes a true statement about China. It is informative, and the statement as such does not make China one of the four ancient civilizations. By contrast, the judge's sentence in Sentence 4) attains the immediate effect of making the man imprisoned. In other words, the words said constitute an act in itself, given the right context. These are what we mean by speech acts, i.e. actions performed via utterances. Other typical ones include thanking, apology, request, compliment, invitation, promise, congratulations, and etc. Performatives are mostly ritualized, and there are conditions for them to be felicitous. The FELICITOUS CONDITIONS suggested by Austin (Austin, 1962: 14–15) are as follows:

A. There must be a relevant conventional procedure, and the relevant participants and circumstances must be appropriate.

B. The procedure must be executed correctly and completely.

C. The relevant people must have the requisite thoughts, feelings and intentions, and must follow it up with actions as specified.

Austin's dichotomy between constatives and performatives makes the ritualized expressions for making social exchanges prominent. Yet, he later realized his mistakes because all utterances can be used to do things. Some may be direct or ritualized in form of expression, and others may be expressed in indirect or implicit ways. For example, "*It is cold here.*" as an indirect request for warming up the room, "*I shall be there.*" as an indirect promise. This is what Searle (1979) later termed "indirect speech act". Such utterances abound in daily communication. People express indirectly for various reasons, like avoiding bluntness, reducing imposition, creating humor, and etc.

Now, one thing that seems at least a fair guess, even from the elaboration of the linguistic construction, as also from its nature in the explicit performative is this: that historically, from the point of view of the evolution of language, the explicit performative must be a later development than certain more primary utterances, many of which at least are already implicit performatives, which are included in most or many explicit performatives as parts of a whole. For example, "I will ···" is earlier than "I promise that I will ···". The plausible view would be that in primitive languages it would not yet be clear, it would not yet be possible to distinguish, which of various things that (using later distinctions) we might be doing we were in fact doing. For example, *"Bull"* or *"Thunder"*in a primitive language of one-word utterances could be a warning, information, a prediction, etc. ··· The explicit performative formula, moreover, is only the last and "most successful" of numerous speech devices which have always been used with greater or less success to perform the same function (just as measurement or standardization was the most successful device ever invented for developing *precision* of speech) (Austin, 1962: 71–73).

6.4.2 A Theory of Locutionary Act, Illocutionary Act and Perlocutionary Act

According to Austin (1962: 108), while making an utterance, we are performing three acts simultaneously: "by saying we perform a *locutionary act*, which is roughly equivalent to uttering a certain sentence with a certain sense and reference, which again is roughly equivalent to 'meaning' in the traditional sense. Second, we said that we also perform *illocutionary acts* such as informing, ordering, warning, undertaking, etc., i.e. utterances which have a certain (conventional) force. That is the behavioral aspect of an utterance involving the intention of the speaker, i.e. the act of doing something or having someone do something. Thirdly, we may also perform *perlocutionary acts*: what we bring about or achieve by saying something, that is the consequences of an utterance, such as convincing, persuading, deterring, and even, say, surprising or misleading. "

The performance of an "illocutionary" act can be explained *in* saying something as opposed to performance of an act *of* saying something; and Austin refers to the doctrine of the different types of function of language here in question as the doctrine of *"illocutionary forces"*. The illocutionary act is a conventional act: an act done as conforming to a convention. Thus, ILLOCUTIONARY FORCE may be interpreted as equivalent to speaker's intention, speaker meaning or contextual meaning. The perlocutionary act may include what in a way are consequences (Austin, 1962: 99–107). The following formulas show the relationship between the three acts:

"In saying X I was doing Y" or "I did Y".

"By saying X I did Y" or "I was doing Y".

The former (in) for picking out verbs which are names for illocutionary acts, and the latter (by) for picking out verbs which are names for perlocutionary acts. For example: "In saying *I would shoot him* I was threatening him". "By saying *I would shoot him* I alarmed him". Austin sees using "by" indicates its "means–to–end" meaning which is different from "in", so he confines "by" in the formula of perlocutionary acts (Austin, 1962: 121–138). For example,

In saying "I will come tomorrow", I was making a promise.

By saying "I will come tomorrow" and making a promise, I reassure my friends.

6.4.3 Classification of Speech Acts

According to Searle (1979: 12–17), there are five basic categories of illocutionary acts: assertives, directives, commissives, expressives, and declarations.

Assertives or representatives are those kinds of speech acts that state what speakers believe to be the case or not, covering claims, reports, descriptions, assertions, conclusions, etc. (Yule, 1996: 53). For example, *I'm specialized in linguistics. The weather in South China is hot and rainy at this time.*

Directives are those kinds of speech acts that speakers perform to get someone else to do something, covering such acts as commands, orders, requests, suggestions, etc. (Yule, 1996: 54). For example, *Please keep quiet. Come on, guys!*

Commissives are those kinds of speech acts that speakers perform to commit themselves to some future action, such as promises, threats, refusals, and offers (Yule, 1996: 54). For example, *Don't harass me or I'll call the police. I'll take you to the movie tonight.*

Expressives are those kinds of speech acts that speakers perform to state their psychological states, such as pleasure, pain, likes, dislikes, joy, or sorrow (Yule, 1996: 53). For example, *Congratulations! I'm terribly sorry.*

Declarations or declaratives are those kinds of speech acts that speakers perform to change the world via their utterance (Yule, 1996: 53). Typical declarations include dismissing (an employee), declaring (a war), nominating (a candidate), naming (a ship), marrying (a couple), etc. These acts are generally governed by social conventions in the course of their execution. The language used is often formulaic. For example, *I now pronounce you husband and wife. I declare the opening of the first international Olympic Games in Athens.*

Searle states that politeness is one of the primary reasons for using an indirect speech act. It is worth mentioning that we can perform one category of speech act, e.g. a representative act like the description of one's hunger in order to perform another, e.g. a directive act like a request to get someone to bring the speaker some food, resulting in an indirect speech act. An indirect speech act (Searle, 1975) can be defined as an utterance in which one illocutionary act (the primary act) is intentionally performed by means of the performance of another act (the literal act). For example, the Nigerian professor Ozidi Bariki describes a conversation in which he said to a friend:

"I love your left hand." (The friend had a cup of tea in his hand). The friend, in reaction to my utterance, transferred the cup to his right hand. That prompted me to say: "I love your right hand". My friend smiled, recognized my desire for tea and told his sister, "My friend wants tea"… My friend's utterance addressed to his sister in reaction to mine was a representative, i.e. a simple statement: "my friend wants tea". The girl rightly interpreted the context of the representative to mean a directive. In other words, her brother (my friend) was ordering her to prepare some tea. (Bariki, 2008)

This brief dialogue contains two examples of indirect speech acts. In both cases, the utterance has the form of a simple statement, but is actually intended to perform a different kind of act: request in the first case and command in the second. The second statement, "My friend wants tea," was immediately and automatically interpreted correctly by the addressee. (In African culture, when an older brother makes such a statement to his younger sister, there is only one possible interpretation.) The first statement, however, failed to communicate. Only after the second attempt was the addressee able to work out the intended meaning, not automatically at all, but as if he was trying to solve a riddle (10.3: Indirect speech acts, https://socialsci.libretexts.org/).

Searle's classification of illocutionary act mainly explains the speaker meaning, while it does not consider the hearer's response. Verbal communication is realized by means of dialogues between a speaker and a hearer. This starts the conversation analysis.

6.5 Theory of Conversational Implicature

The second major theory in pragmatics is the theory of conversational implicature, proposed by another Oxford philosopher Herbert Paul Grice. Grice began to formulate his theory in the 1950s, but it was through his William James lectures on "Logic and Conversation" delivered at Harvard in 1967 that this theory became known to the public. His seminal paper was published in 1975 as a chapter in Volume 3 of *Syntax and Semantics: Speech Acts*.

6.5.1 The Notion of Implicature

In the beginning of his paper "Logic and Conversation", Grice points out a fact that in our daily conversation (communication), a speaker's meaning which Grice called "conversational implicatures" are nonconventional (not the conventional meaning of the uttered sentence). He tries to summarize the features of "conversational implicature" through Cooperative Principle and its four maxims (Grice, 1967: 26).

According to Grice, conversational implicatures may be of two types: generalized conversational implicatures and particularized implicatures.

The former require no special contextual information on the part of the hearer to make the inference; whereas the latter require the hearer to have the relevant background knowledge of the particular context involved. The generalized conversational implicatures are normally carried by the use of a certain lexical item or expression, in the absence of special circumstances. For example:

9) I received a party invitation from *a gentleman*.

10) Elizabeth has collected *some* of the artist's paintings.

11) Mary has *three* children.

Example 9) implies that the gentleman is not the female speaker's husband. Example 10) implies that Elizabeth has not collected all of the artist's paintings. And Example 11) implies that Mary has only three children. So there may be a generalized conversational implicature from an expression with an indefinite article like *a gentleman* which is not closely related to the speaker, a scalar quantity expression like *some* which implicates that a higher or stronger point on the scale is not obtained, and a number like *three* which means no more or no less than itself.

In contrast, particularized implicatures arise only in a particular context of utterance. For example:

12) Mary: What on earth has happened to the roast beef?

Jack: The dog is looking very happy.

In the above exchange, Mary will likely get the implicature "the dog ate the roast beef" from Jack's statement. This is due to Mary's belief that Jack is observing the conversational maxim of relation or relevance in the specific context of Mary's question.

In "Logic and Conversation", Grice mentions some characteristics of conversational implicature. We summarize Grice's ideas in the light of other linguists' elaborations as follows:

A.Calculability

Conversational implicatures can be worked out on the basis of the conventional meaning of the sentences, together with the CP and its maxims, and the specific context of the utterance.

B.Cancellability

Conversational implicatures relies on the conventional meaning of the sentences uttered, the CP, and specific contexts. So, if any of them changes, the implicature will also change.

C.Non−Detachability

Non−detachability means that a conversational implicature is attached to the semantic content of what is said, not to the linguistic form. Thus, conversational implicatures do not vanish if the expressions of an utterance are changed for synonyms.

D.Non−Conventionality

Conversational implicature is by definition different from the conventional meaning of the expressions. It is context−dependent and varies with context.

6.5.2 Cooperative Principle and Its Maxims

In the beginning of "Logic and Conversation", Grice points out that native speakers almost intuitively arrive at conversational implicature like Mary in Example 12). However, a theory needs to make it explicit how this implicature is derived. Grice's solution is the assumption of the Cooperative Principle (CP) at work in daily verbal communication. Grice introduces the principle as follows: Make your conversational contribution such as is required, at the stage at which it occurs, by the accepted purpose or direction of the talk exchange in which you are engaged (Grice, 1967: 26–27). In order to explain the mechanisms by which people interpret conversational implicature, Grice(1967: 26–27) introduces four maxims under the CP as follows:

Quantity:

1.Make your contribution as informative as required (for the current purposes of the exchange).

2.Do not make your contribution more informative than required.

Quality:

1.Do not say what you believe to be false.

2.Do not say that for which you lack adequate evidence.

Relation: Be relevant.

Manner: Be perspicuous.

1.Avoid obscurity of expression.

2.Avoid ambiguity.

3.Be brief（avoid unnecessary prolixity).

4.Be orderly .

It is worth mentioning that CP with its four maxims is not something that prescribes how people should talk in conversation. It specifies what participants have to do in order to talk in a maximally efficient, cooperative way. It is an assumption of the principle we uphold in conversations. We assume that people normally abide by these maxims in conversations. In some cases, these maxims are fully observed, which will not give rise to implicatures; but in other cases, they are not fully observed, which will result in implicatures.

6.5.3 Flouting the Maxims

There are two major types of violation of CP and its maxims. The first type is the total ignorance or rejection of CP and its maxims. This may take an explicit form, such as *No comment* or *I don't want to talk about it*, or an implicit form, e.g. the speakers tell lies to mislead or deceive the hearers.

The second type is that the speaker fails to fulfill one maxim while still observing the general principle. There may be two reasons. One reason is that the speaker may face a conflict of maxims. For example,

13) A: Where does Mike live?

B: Somewhere in the South of France.

In this example, B would infringe the Maxim of Quality if B risks being as informative as is required in the absence of enough information. The solution is to strike a balance between the two, as shown in B's answer.

The other reason is that the speaker wants to convey some conversational implicature. The solution is to openly flout/ ignore some maxim. The following are conversational exchanges that involve openly flouting some maxims:

14) Dear Sir,

Mr. X's command of English is excellent, and his attendance at tutorials has been regular.

Yours

15) Aunt: How did Jimmy do his history exam?

Mother: Oh, not at all well. Teachers asked him things that happened before the poor boy was born.

16) You are the cream in my coffee.

17) A: Mrs. X is an old bag.

B: The weather has been quite delightful this summer, hasn't it?

18) A: Let's get the kids something.

B: Ok, but I veto I–C–E–C–R–E–A–M.

In the above exchanges, Example 14) presents violation of Maxim of Quantity, in which a philosophy teacher is writing a recommendation letter for his pupil who is a candidate for a philosophy job. As a teacher, he knows that more information than this is wanted. By such a letter he implies Mr. X is not good at philosophy. In Example 15), the mother's answer gives more information than required to the aunt's question, violating the Maxim of Quantity. Her answer implies that her son should not be blamed. Example 16) violates the Maxim of Quality, which intends to mean "You are my pride and joy". In Example 17), B violates the Maxim of Relation and diverges the topic from *Mr. X* to *weather*, openly refusing to make what he says relevant to A's remark. He implies that A's remark should not be discussed. And in Example 18), B violates the Maxim of Manner. B uses a big word "veto" which is probably unintelligible to the kids, and B also pronounces the familiar word ice-cream in a way that may again baffle the kids. In this way, B implies "Don't give them ice-cream".

It is worth mentioning that it is the specific context that counts in hearer's making inference to get the speaker's conversational implicature. So, it is important for second language learners to enhance their knowledge of target-language culture in order to make better intercultural communications.

6.6 Politeness Principle

Grice's Cooperative Principle and its maxims explain the speaker's conversational implicature on the basis of the literal meaning of the utterance, CP and contexts. It is logic-oriented. But it does not explain why people tend to flout some maxims in order to convey their intentions (i.e. speak indirectly rather than directly) in daily communication. Geoffrey Neil Leech (16 January, 1936 – 19 August, 2014), who was a Fellow of the British Academy, an Honorary Fellow of UCL and of Lancaster University, provides the answer through Politeness Principle: conversation is in nature a social exchange, in which people need to talk politely to maintain a comfortable relationship.

6.6.1 Politeness Principle and Its Maxims

In its negative form, the PP might be formulated in a general way:"Minimize (other things being equal) the expression of impolite beliefs;" and there is a corresponding positive version "Maximize (other things being equal) the expression of polite beliefs" which is somewhat less important (Leech, 1983: 81).

According to Leech, as a general point, that politeness concerns a relationship between two participants whom we may call *self* and *other*. If there is benefit, there must be cost. The offer and invitation are presumed to be polite for two reasons: firstly, because they imply benefit to *other*, and secondly and less crucially, because they imply cost to *self*. For other acts like a request, an order and a demand are considered impolite, because they imply cost to *other*.

Specifically, the principle is composed of six maxims:

A.Tact Maxim: Minimize cost to other; Maximize benefit to other.

For example:

19) Could I interrupt you for *a second*?

20) *Could you please* tell me how to get to the London Tower?

21) Have a good time this evening!

22) Enjoy your holiday.

The first part of Tact Maxim fits in with Leech's negative politeness strategy of minimizing the imposition, and the second part reflects the positive politeness strategy of attending to the *other*'s needs, wants and interests. Examples 19) and 20) are indirect ways to make a request. A polite speaker may use minimizers such as *a second, could you please* to reduce the implied cost to the *other*. Thus Examples 19) and 20) offer *others* (hearers) certain alternative to decide whether or not they will do what is imposed. It is less impolite for hearers to refuse such requests. Conversely, if we keep the imperative mood constant to get a hearer (*other*) to do what is to his benefit, there is a general increase in politeness, such as Examples 21) and 22).

B.Generosity Maxim: Minimize benefit to self; Maximize cost to self.

For example:

23) Could I borrow this electric drill?

24) You relax and let me do the dishes.

25) I can lend you my car.

26) You must come and have dinner with us.

Unlike the tact maxim, the maxim of generosity focuses on *self* (the speaker), and says that *others* should be put first instead of the *self*. Example 23) is more polite than *Could you lend me this electric drill?* This is because the illocutionary goal of Example 23) overtly compete with the Generosity Maxim, but not with the Tact Maxim (Leech, 1983: 134). And the offer of Example 24), 25) and invitation of Example 26) are presumed to be polite because they imply to benefit to the hearers (*others*) and they imply cost to *self*.

C.Approbation Maxim: Minimize dispraise of other; Maximize praise of other.

For example:

27) A: Her performance was outstanding!

   B: Yes, wasn't it!

28) Gideon, I know you're a genius—would you know how to solve this math problem here?

29) You could be more careful.

30) A: Do you like these apricots?

   B: I've tasted better.

It is preferred to praise others and if this is impossible, to sidestep the issue, to give some sort of minimal response (possibly through the use of euphemisms), or to remain silent. The first part of the maxim avoids disagreement; the second part intends to make other people feel good by showing solidarity. Examples 27) and 28) maximize praise of others; while Examples 29) and 30) implies reluctance to criticize the others in institutionalized forms of understatement. Leech mentions that Grice's example of the philosophy teacher's recommendation letter to his pupil just implies the teacher (*self*)'s reluctance to declare his opinion is due to the Approbation Maxim (Leech, 1983: 136).

D.Modesty Maxim: Minimize praise of self; Maximize dispraise of self. For example:

31) Oh, I'm so stupid – I didn't make a note of our lecture! Did you?

32) How clever of you!

Example 31) shows how self-dispraise is regarded as quite benign, even when it is exaggerated for comic effect.

E.Agreement Maxim: Minimize disagreement between self and other;

Maximize agreement between self and other.

For example:

33) A: A referendum will satisfy everybody.

　　B: Yes, definitely.

34) A: I don't want my daughter to do this, I want her to do that.

　　B: Yes, but ma'am, I thought we resolved this already on your last visit.

35) A: English is a difficult language to learn.

　　B: True, but the grammar is quite easy.

It is in line with leech's positive politeness strategies of "seek agreement" and "avoid disagreement", to which they attach great importance. However, it is not being claimed that people totally avoid disagreement. It is simply observed that they are much more direct in expressing agreement, rather than disagreement. Examples 34) and 35) show, partial disagreement is often preferable to complete disagreement.

F.Sympathy Maxim: Minimize antipathy between self and other; Maximize sympathy between self and other.

For example:

36) I am sorry to hear about your father.

Sympathy Maxim includes a small group of speech acts such as congratulations and condolences － all of which are in accordance with Leech's positive politeness strategy of attending to the hearer's interests, wants, and needs.

6.6.2 Contrast of Chinese and English

索振羽认为，"礼貌"是有明显的民族性的：这个民族认为是"礼貌"的，另一个民族也许认为是"不礼貌"的；这个民族认为是"不礼貌"的，另一个民族也许认为是"礼貌的"。例如，*X: Oh, What beautiful handwriting! Y: No, no, not at all. You are joking! (X* 英国女教师，*Y* 中国女学生 *)*。但是，不论东方文化还是西方文化，每个民族都是提倡礼貌，重视礼貌的，这是共性。中华民族有五千年文明史，人称"礼仪之邦"，一向重视人际交往的礼貌，在言语交际中使用尊重交谈对象、表示友好的礼貌语言。当前的中国，正处在国家现代化建设时期，更应该重视礼貌。在当前，研究"礼貌准则"，在言语交际中提倡并遵守"礼貌准则"，对促进社会主义精神文明建设有重要的理论意义和现实意义（索，2000: 90）。

索振羽认为："得体"应从利奇礼貌原则中提升至高层次。因为从言语交际的根本目的看，语用交际中的礼貌原则是为了话语的得体，但话语得体不是为了礼貌。除了利奇所提，索振羽认为"得体原则"包括礼貌准则、幽默准则、克制准则（索，2000: 90–123）。

礼貌准则：除了原利奇礼貌原则下的五个准则（提出得体准则），还包括"恰当的称呼次准则"。称呼语代表人与人之间的一种社会关系。视尊卑、长幼、亲疏之不同，在交际中对听话人使用恰当的称呼也是一种礼貌，如 "*触犯了国家法律的年轻的朋友们！* "礼貌准则案例如：

一语未完，只听后院中有笑语声，说："我来迟了，没得迎接远客！"黛玉思忖道："这些人个个皆敛声屏气如此，这来者是谁，这样放诞无礼？……"心下想时，只见一群媳妇丫鬟拥着一个丽人从后房门进来。这个人打扮与姑娘们不同：彩绣辉煌，恍若神妃仙子。头上戴着金丝八宝攒珠髻，绾着朝阳五凤挂珠钗；项上戴着赤金盘螭璎珞圈；身上穿着缕金百蝶穿花大红洋缎窄裉袄，外罩五彩刻丝石青银鼠褂；下着翡翠撒花洋绉裙。一双丹凤三角眼，两弯柳叶吊梢眉。身量苗条，体格风骚。粉面含春威不露，丹唇未启笑先闻。

黛玉连忙起身接见。贾母笑道："你不认得他。他是我们这里有名的一个泼皮破落户儿，南省俗谓作'辣子'，你只叫他'凤辣子'就是了。"黛玉正不知以何称呼，众姊妹都忙告诉黛玉道："这是琏二嫂子。"黛玉虽不曾识面，听见他母亲说过："大舅贾赦之子贾琏娶的就是二舅母王氏的内侄女，自幼假充男儿教养，学名叫做王熙凤。"黛玉忙陪笑见礼，以"嫂"呼之。

这熙凤携着黛玉的手，上下细细打量一回，便仍送至贾母身边坐下，因笑道："天下真有这样标致人儿！我今日才算看见了！况且这通身的气派竟不像老祖宗的外孙女儿，竟是个嫡亲的孙女儿似的。怨不得老祖宗天天嘴里心里放不下。——只可怜我这妹妹这么命苦：怎么姑妈偏就去世了呢！"说着，便用手帕拭泪。贾母笑道："我才好了，你又来招我。你妹妹远路才来，身子又弱，也才劝住了。快别再提了。"——曹雪芹《红楼梦》第三回

曹雪芹一开始就让我们见识到王熙凤的口才。当时来迎接林黛玉的人很多，贾母、邢夫人、王夫人、贾迎春、贾探春、贾惜春等都在场。王熙凤说话主要针对新来的客人林黛玉，但又不能冷落了其他人。王熙凤的话有以下几层会话含义：一、赞美了林黛玉。林黛玉是新来的，又是第一次见面，而且她确实长得标致，所以这个赞美是理所当然的，也是当之无愧的。对于王熙凤来说，这也是直话直说，没有夸张。二、

奉承了贾母。贾母最为年长，贾政、王夫人、邢夫人都得贤孝她，包括王熙凤这个侄孙媳妇。孙女也好，外孙女也好，都是贾母有血缘的后代。赞扬贾母子孙，贾母当然高兴。三、夸赞了在座的迎春、探春和惜春，即王熙凤的小姑子们。凤姐不是独夸林黛玉、贬低三姐妹，而是夸赞林黛玉跟三姊妹一样长得漂亮。所以三春在旁边不会尴尬，而是觉得舒服。

可以说，王熙凤的这段话，夸了林黛玉，夸了贾母，也夸了在座的贾迎春、贾探春和贾惜春，也表达了自己对林黛玉的心疼，说得相当礼貌、得体而精彩。

幽默准则：得体的话语并不都是礼貌的，如幽默话语，但不能说它不得体，因为适合特定环境，幽默话语的交际效果最佳。幽默可以增添欢乐、消除隔阂、缓解矛盾、显示才智、摆脱困境、回敬挑衅。语言中幽默存在的形式也很多，如语言类节目、修辞、熟语（习语、歇后语）、脑筋急转弯。例如：

1.Customer: Waiter! There's a fly in the soup.

Waiter: Don't worry. There is no extra charge.

2.一对新婚夫妇发生争吵,妻子哭着闹着要跟丈夫分手回到娘家去。

妻子(哭着)："我要回娘家,你把车费给我。"

丈夫(无奈)："好吧。亲爱的,这是你回家的车费。"

妻子数了数钱后,看到丈夫无奈又痛苦的表情,不免心软,随后又说："那,你把我回来的车费也给我啊。"

3. 阿凡提和国王的一次对话：

国王："阿凡提,如果在你的这边放着金子,在那边放着真理,你要哪一样呢？"

阿凡提："陛下，我要金子。"

国王："多蠢呀，阿凡提！金银财宝算得了什么，而要得到真理可就不容易了。我如果是你的话，是要选择真理的。"

阿凡提："陛下，您的话对极了，谁缺少什么就要什么，咱们各得其所呀！"

4. 陈毅外长在一次记者招待会上：

西方某记者："中国是用什么武器把美国的 U-2 型飞机击落的？"

陈外长："是用竹竿捅下来的。"

在当时，用什么武器击落入侵我国的美国 U-2 型高空侦察机是国家机密。西方记者的提问给陈外长出了个大难题。陈外长幽默地回答"是用竹竿捅下来的"，既严格地保守了国家机密，又大大活跃了记者招待会的气氛，在一片笑声中摆脱了困境，这充分显示出陈外长高超的外交艺术。

5. 周恩来总理在一次记者招待会上：

西方记者："请问中国人民银行有多少资金？"

周总理："中国人民银行货币资金有 18 元 8 角 8 分。"

在场全体记者愕然。

周总理："中国人民银行发行面额为 10 元、5 元、2 元、1 元、5 角、2 角、1 角、5 分、2 分、1 分，共 10 种主辅人民币，合计为 18 元 8 角 8 分。中国人民银行是中国人民当家作主的金融机构，有全国人民做后盾，信用卓著，实力雄厚，它所发行的货币是世界上最有信誉的一种货币，在国际上享有盛誉。"

这里，周总理巧妙地把中国人民银行的"资金总额"转换成中国人民银行"发行货币的面额"，运用"中国人民银行货币有 18 元 8

角8分"这句幽默话语，既保守了国家机密，又增添了记者招待会的活跃气氛，表现出周总理超群的才智和外交才能。

克制准则：在言语交际中，说话人由于种种原因（如不便直言或不能直言等）不直言不讳地训斥他人，而采用克制的方式表达对他人的不满或责备。比如：讽刺挖苦、指桑骂槐、反语。例如：

（贾赦）因说道："一家子一个儿子最孝顺。偏生母亲病了，各处求医不得，便请了一个针灸的婆子来。这婆子原不知道脉理，只说是心火，如今用针灸之法，针灸针灸就好了。这儿子慌了，便问：'心见铁就死，如何针得？'婆子道：'不用针心，只针肋条就是了。'儿子道，'肋条离心远着呢，怎么就好？'婆子道：'不妨事。你不知天下父母心偏的多呢。'"众人听说，都笑起来。贾母也只得吃半杯酒，半日笑道："我也得这婆子针一针就好了。"贾赦听说，自知出言冒撞，贾母疑心，忙起身笑与贾母把盏，以别言解释。——曹雪芹《红楼梦》第七十五回

贾赦倚官作势，行为不检，甚至打起了贾母丫头鸳鸯的主意。此事被贾母回绝后，贾赦羞愧难当，不敢面见贾母，每日请安打发邢夫人代劳。贾赦同时也不满母亲偏向弟弟贾政，因此在中秋夜宴上，借讲笑话之机，发泄对母亲的怨恨。贾母心知肚明，但又不好发怒。人家又没有明说是你，你如果挑明，不是对号入座，自取其辱吗？如果一点"反应"也没有，不又显得怯懦和木讷了吗？对此，贾母"以其人之道还治其人之身"，含蓄地表明自己的想法。贾母的这一招果然奏效，贾赦忙起身笑与贾母把盏，以别言解释。从贾母克制的言语中，我们不难看出贾母的聪明才智和非凡的应变能力，既不伤儿子的情面，又维护了自己的尊严，同时也不破坏宴会和谐的气氛。此后贾母也没

有再提及此事，体现出贾母"拿得起，放得下"的优秀品质。总之，在这件事上，贾母始终都很克制，事态把握得恰到好处，体现出一个长者的气度、博大胸怀和非凡的应变能力。

6.7 Summary

To make a summary of this brief and incomplete introduction to pragmatics, firstly it is worth mentioning that pragmatics sees that we use language to perform speech acts: the utterance itself, the conveying of our intention in the utterance and the consequence brought by the utterance. That is a difference between pragmatics and semantics. The speaker's intention is always beyond the literal meaning of the uttered expressions. Grice's Cooperative Principle and its maxims explains how a speaker coneys his intention (the conversational implicature) through observing or flouting CP and its maxims. CP is logic-oriented. According to Leech, Politeness Principle is another mechanism employed to work out conversational implicature. But it is from sociological and psychological point of views. Since conversation is in nature a social exchange, Politeness Principle and its maxims are supposed to collaborate with or even to rescue the Cooperative Principle in interpreting indirectness of conversation. Since pragmatics is a newly-developed branch of linguistics, and it concerns the study of language from the viewpoint of the users, especially the choices they make, the constraints they encounter in using language in social interaction, and the effects their use of language has on other participants in an act of communication (Crystal, 1985: 240). There are various other classic principles explaining the use of language in this field, such as Relevance Theory proposed by Sperber and Wilson (1986), and Conversation Analysis (CA) proposed by Sacks, Schegloff and Jefferson (1974). All these need a further reading.

Further Readings:

Austin, J.L. 1975. *How to Do Things with Words 2nd ed.* Oxford: Clarendon Press. Reprinted in China by 外语教学与研究出版社, 2002.

Grice, H.P. 1975. *Logic and Conversation.* In Grice, P. (ed.) 1989/2002. *Studies in the Way of Words.* 北京 : 外语教学与研究出版社 .

Leech, G.N. 1983. *Principles of Pragmatics.* London: Longman.

Levinson, S.C. 1983. *Pragmatics.* Cambridge: Cambridge University Press.

索振羽 , 2000. 《语用学教程》. 北京 : 北京大学出版社 .

Sperber, D. & Wilson, D. 1986. *Relevance: Communication and Cognition.* Oxford: Blackwell. Reprinted in China by 外语教学与研究出版社 , 2002.

Yule, G. 1996. *Pragmatics.* 上海 : 上海外语教育出版社 .

Questions and Exercises:

1.Define the following terms:

constatives, performatives, speech act, locutionary act, illocutionary act, perlocutionary act, indirect speech act, Searle's five types of illocutionary speech acts, Cooperative Principle, conversational implicature, Politeness Principle

2.How are syntax and semantics related to pragmatics?

3.Perlocutionary acts may sometimes fail to obtain the effect intended by the speaker. Explain what may have led to the failure.

4.Find more examples to illustrate how conversational implicature is generated through the flouting of conversational maxims.

5.Find examples to illustrate Politeness between Chinese and Western cultures.

References

Adams, V. 1973. *An Introduction to Modern English Word–Formation*. London: Longman.

Aitchison, J. 1992. *Teach Yourself Linguistics*. London: Hodder & Stoughton.

Austin, J.L. 1962/ 1975. *How to Do Things with Words 2nd ed.* Oxford: Clarendon Press.

Bariki, Ozidi. 2008. *"On the relationship between translation and pragmatics". International Journal of Translation(Vol. 20, Issue 1–2).* New Delhi: Bahri Publications.

Bauer, Laurie. 1983. *English Word–Formation*. London: Cambridge University Press.

Bloch, B. & Trager, G. L. 1942. *Outline of Linguistic Analysis*. Baltimore: Linguistics Society of America/ Waverly Press.

Bloomfield, Leonard. 1933/2002. *Language*. 北京：外语教学与研究出版社.

Boas, F. 1911. *Handbook of American Indian Languages*. Washington, D.

C.: Smithonian Institution.

Brinton, Laurel J. 2000. *The Structure of Modern English: A Linguistic Introduction*. Amsterdam, Philadelphia: John Benjamins.

Brown, P. & Levinson, S. C. 1987. *Politeness: Some Universals in Language Usage*. Cambridge: Cambridge University Press.

Carstairs–McCarthy, A. 2002. *An Introduction to English Morphology: Words and Their Structure*. Edinburgh: Edinburgh University Press.

Chomsky, N. 1957. *Syntactic Structures.* The Hague: Mouton.

Chomsky, N. 1965. *Aspects of the Theory of Syntax*. Cambridge, Mass: MIT Press.

Chomsky, N. 1986. *Barriers.* Cambridge, Mass: MIT Press.

Chomsky, N. 1995. *The Minimalist Program.* Cambridge, Mass: MIT Press.

Clark, John &Colin, Yallop. 1995. *An Introduction to Phonetics and Phonology*. 2nd ed. Oxford: Blackwell. (Reprinted by Foreign Language Teaching and Research Press in 2000)

Cook, V. 2000. *Chomsky's Universal Grammar 2nd Edition*. Beijing: Foreign Language Teaching and Research Press.

Cruttenden, A. 1997. *Intonation 2nd Edition.* Cambridge: Cambridge University Press.

Crystal, D. 1985. *A dictionary of linguistics and phonetics 2nd Edition.* Oxford: Blackwell.

Crystal, D. 1992/1997. *The Cambridge Encyclopedia of Language*. Cambridge: Cambridge University Press.

Eggins, S. 1994. *An Introduction to Systemic Functional Linguistics.* London: Pinter.

Gimson, A. C. & Alan Cruttenden. 2001. *Gimson's Pronunciation of English*. 6th ed. London: Arnold. (Reprinted by Foreign Language Teaching and Research Press in 2001)

Grice, H.P. 1967. *Logic and Conversation.* In Grice, P. (ed.) 1989/2002. *Studies in the Way of Words.* 北京 : 外语教学与研究出版社 .

Halliday, M. A. K. 1985/1994/2008. *An Introduction to Functional Grammar.* 北京 : 外语教学与研究出版社 .

Halliday, M. A. K. & Hasan, R. 1976/2001. *Cohesion in English*. 北京 : 外语教学与研究出版社 .

Halliday, M. A. K. 1990. *"New Ways of Meaning: The Challenge to Applied Linguistics"* in *Journal of Applied Linguistics, 6, Ninth World Congress of Applied Linguistics Special Issue*. Thessaloniki: The Greek Applied Linguistics Association (GALA).

Hockett, C. F. 1958. *A Course in Modern Linguistics*. New York: Macmillan.

Jakobson, R. 1960. *"Linguistics and Poetry"* in *Style and Language*, ed. Sebeok, T.A. Cambridge Mass: MIT Press.

Jones, Daniel. 1962. *Outline of English Phonetics*. Cambridge: Heffer.

Katz, J. J. and Fodor, J. A. 1963. *"The Structure of a Semantic Theory"*. In *Language*, 39: 170–210. (Reprinted in Rosenberg, J.F. & Travis, C. eds., 1971. *Readings in the Philosophy of Language*, 472–514. New Jersey: Prentice Hall, Inc.)

Kenneth, D. J. 2003. *"Temporal constraints and characterizing syllable structuring"*. In Local, John; Ogden, Richard; Temple, Rosalind (eds.). *Phonetic Interpretation: Papers in Laboratory Phonology VI*. Cambridge: Cambridge University Press.

Leech, G. 1981. *Semantics: The Study of Meaning,2nd ed.* Harmondsworth: Penguin.

Leech, G.N. 1983. *Principles of Pragmatics.* London: Longman.

Lehrer, Adrienne. 1985. "*The Influence of Semantic Fields on Semantic Change*". In Fisiak, J. (ed), *Historical Semantics. Historical Word-formation*. Berlin: Mouton.

Levinson, S.C. 1983. *Pragmatics.* Cambridge: Cambridge University Press.

Lyons, J. 1977. *Semantics, 2 vols*. Cambridge: Cambridge University Press.

Lyons, John. 1981. *Language and Linguistics*. Cambridge: Cambridge University Press.

Lyons, J. 1995/2000. *Linguistic Semantics: An Introduction.* 北京：外语教学与研究出版社.

Matthews, P. H. 1981. *Syntax.* Cambridge: Cambridge University Press.

Matthews, P.H. 2000. *Morphology (2nd Edition).* 北京：外语教学与研究出版社.

Malinowski, B. 1923. *The Problem of Meaning in Primitive Language*, supplement to C. K. Ogden and I. A. Richards. *The Meaning of Meaning*. London: Routledge & Kegan Paul.

Morris, C. 1938. *Foundations of the Theory of Signs*. Chicago: University of Chicago Press.

Ogden, C.K. & Richards, I.A. 1923. *The Meaning of Meaning*. London: Routledge & Kegan Paul.

Radford, A. et al. 2000. *Linguistics: An Introduction*. 北京：外语教学与研究出版社.

Roach, Peter. 2000. *English Phonetics and Phonology: A Practical Course*. 3rd Edition. Cambridge: Cambridge University Press. (Second edition reprinted by Foreign Language Teaching and Research Press in 2000)

Roach, Peter. 2001. *Phonetics*. Oxford: Oxford University Press. (Reprinted by Shanghai Foreign Language Education Press in 2003)

Robins, R. H. 1959. *"In defense of WP"*. TPhS. 116 - 144.Google Scholar.

Sacks, H., Schegloff, E. A., & Jefferson, G. 1974. *"A Simplest Systematics for the Organization of Turn-taking for Conversation"*. Language, 50(4), 696-735.

Saeed, J. I. 2009. *Semantics 3rd ed.* 北京：外语教学与研究出版社.

Sapir, E. 1921/ 2002. *Language*. 北京：外语教学与研究出版社.

Saussure, F. D. 1916/2002. *Course in General Linguistics*. 北京：外语教学与研究出版社.

Searle, J. 1979. *Expression and Meaning: Studies in the Theory of Speech Acts*. Cambridge: Cambridge University Press.

Searle, J. 1975. *"Indirect Speech Acts"*. In P. Cole & J. L. Morgan (Eds.),

Syntax and Semantics (vol. 3, pp.59–82). New York: Academic Press.

Spencer, Andrew. 1996/1999. *Phonology: Theory and Description.* Oxford: Blackwell.

Sperber, D. & Wilson, D. 1986. *Relevance: Communication and Cognition.* Oxford: Blackwell. Reprinted in China by 外语教学与研究出版社, 2002.

Stockwell, R. & Minkova, D. 2001. English Words: History and Structure. Cambridge: Cambridge University Press.

Textor, Mark. 2011. *Frege on Sense and Reference.* London and New York: Routledge.

Thompson, A. et al. 2000. *Introducing Functional Grammar 2nd Edition.* 北京：外语教学与研究出版社.

Widdowson, H. G. 1996/2000. *Linguistics.* 上海：上海外语教育出版社.

Wardhaugh, R. 1986/2000. An Introduction to Sociolinguistics. 北京：外语教学与研究出版社.

Yule, G. 1996. *Pragmatics.* 上海：上海外语教育出版社.

Yule, G. 2000. *The Study of Language.* 北京：外语教学与研究出版社.

Yule, G. 2006. *The Study of Language 3rd Edition.* Cambridge: Cambridge University Press.

陈炜湛, 1978. "汉字起源试论",《中山大学学报》第 1 期.

陈望道, 1932/ 1979.《修辞学发凡》. 上海：上海教育出版社.

戴炜栋 & 何兆熊, 2002.《新编简明英语语言学教程》. 上海：上海外语教育出版社.

高天如，1989."评濮之珍著《中国语言学史》"，《复旦学报（社会科学版）》第 1 期.

黄伯荣 & 廖序东，2002.《现代汉语》.北京：高等教育出版社.

胡壮麟、朱永生、张德禄、李战子，2005.《系统功能语言学概论》.北京：北京大学出版社.

李军，2020."乡音无改鬓毛衰"之"衰"字音义的词源学解释"，《汉字汉语研究》第 3 期.

连淑能，1993.《英汉对比研究》.北京：高等教育出版社.

刘海燕，2010."古汉语同义连用的特点"，《宜春学院学报》第 32 卷第 5 期.

罗竹风，1993.《汉语大词典》.上海：汉语大词典出版社.

戚雨村，1992."语言的共性研究和对《马氏文通》的重新评价"，《复印报刊资料（语言文字学）》第 5 期.

石定栩，2002，《乔姆斯基的形式句法》.北京：北京语言大学出版社.

索振羽，2000.《语用学教程》.北京：北京大学出版社.

汪榕培，2013.《英语词汇学》（十一五国家级规划教材）.上海：上海外语教育出版社.

王力，1980/2004/2015.《汉语史稿》.北京：中华书局.

王力，2010.《汉语语音史》.北京：商务印书馆.

王晓斌，2004."现代汉语语义学研究述要"，《南京林业大学学报（人文社会科学版）》第 4 卷第 1 期.

王寅，2011.《英语语义学教程》（十一五国家级规划教材）.北京：高等教育出版社.

徐烱列，1995 /1990.《语义学》第二版.北京：语文出版社.

许慎 , 2012.《说文解字》. 北京 : 中华书局 .

许余龙 , 2010.《对比语言学第 2 版》. 上海 : 上海外语教育出版社 .

荀况 , 2011.《荀子》. 北京 : 中华书局 .

杨信彰 , 2009.《英语词汇学教程》(十一五国家级规划教材). 北京 :
高等教育出版社 .

叶蜚声 & 徐通锵 , 1997.《语言学纲要》. 北京 : 北京大学出版社 .

赵克勤 , 1986. "古汉语反义词浅论",《语文研究》第 3 期 .